# Outside Pitch

## Twenty years of
# BOSTON BASEBALL

## Michael Rutstein

# Outside Pitch

## *Twenty Years of Boston Baseball*

Copyright 2009 by Michael Rutstein

ISBN: 1449524796 EAN-13: 9781449524791
Published 2009 by Pennant Publications, Inc.
73 Middleton Road, Boxford, MA 01921
(978) 561-3020

*This book is for my parents, who always believed in me.*

2016

**CNN Headline News
April 17, 1993**

[Footage of Andre Dawson homering at Fenway Park. Dateline: Boston]

Voiceover: "For 81 years the Boston Red Sox have waged their battles in legendary Fenway Park. But these days, they are also battling outside the park."

[Cut to Harry M. Stevens hawker]

HMS Hawker: Red Sox programs here, one dollar!

"Call it the war of the programs. This is the official program. And this..."

[Cut to *Baseball Underground* hawker]

BU Hawker: Today's lineups! *Baseball Underground*, folks! Just one dollar!

"...is the often critical UNOFFICIAL program, started by this man, [cut to Mike Rutstein, selling magazines] who fancies himself as a modern-day David who the Goliath Red Sox [cut to Fenway Park façade] are trying to squash.

[Cut to Rutstein, up close]

Rutstein: Any time a big company like the Red Sox loses a monopoly they're upset about it, and I think they'd very much like to get 100% of the market back. And I think that's their strategy, is to put us out of business.

[Cut to another HMS hawker]

HMS Hawker: Do not settle for cheap imitations! This is the official one, right here!

"The Red Sox do admit they called Boston Code Enforcement officers last year, who then gave *Baseball Underground*'s publisher a criminal summons for vending without proper licensing. [Cut to Rutstein, making a sale] But were the Red Sox trying to squash his business?"

[Cut to Larry Cancro, on field]

Cancro: That's absolutely untrue.

"Larry Cancro is the Red Sox' Director of Marketing."

Cancro: We were just checking to see if the City had changed their stance on the number of vendors on the street.

[Cut to peanut hawker on Yawkey Way]

Hawker: Fresh roasted peanuts! Cashews, pistachios, hot pretzels! "Amid a cavalcade of outside vendors, *Baseball Underground* says it sells as many as 3,000 programs a game."
[Cut to Fan at Gate A]
Fan: It gives you an option. It's capitalism in action, right behind you, right here!
"But the Red Sox aren't just standing around. While *Baseball Underground* costs one dollar, the Red Sox have decided to change the price of their two-dollar program to..."
HMS Hawker: One dollar!
[Cut to Rutstein]
Rutstein: It's pretty obviously a response to *Baseball Underground*.
[Cut to Cancro]
Cancro: I would say it was in relation to ah... to... to the... the feedback that we received from fans.
"In the meantime, criminal charges have been dropped against *Baseball Underground*'s publisher. He's been told he has a First Amendment right to sell his periodical, so the war of the programs shows no signs of letting up."
[Cut to Cancro]
Cancro: Ours is a slicker magazine style, which is nice...
[Cut to Rutstein]
Rutstein: We come out twice as often...
[Cut to Cancro]
Cancro: It has up-to-date statistical information tucked in...
[Cut to Rutstein]
Rutstein: We give away a free pencil...
"The salespeople for the two publications compete fiercely. The fans here can only hope their team competes just as fiercely.
"Gary Tuchman, CNN, Boston."

During the fall of 2008 I sat down to write a short book about *Boston Baseball*, the magazine I launched back in 1990, when I was 25 years old, and which was about to celebrate its 20th anniversary.

I started by describing a typical day at the ballpark during the just-completed 2008 season, and then turned back the clock to 1990 and told the whole story through, chronologically. I have copies of every magazine we've ever published, and I referred to them constantly as I wrote. I also had a photo album of the various guys (and girls) who have worked for me at the ballpark, and a thick folder of newspaper and magazine clippings.

With these as my primary sources — supplementing a memory that is notoriously bad — I banged out 50,000 words in about six weeks, and considered it a job well done. When it was finished, I cleaned it up and sent it out to several of the guys who have worked for me over the years.

They hated it.

Mostly they hated it because MY story of *Boston Baseball* wasn't THEIR story of *Boston Baseball*. As they made very clear to me, there are many stories here, and none of them is really about how many games the Red Sox won, how many magazines we moved, or how much advertising we sold.

This is a story about pursuing your dream, a story about what you can accomplish through intelligence and hard work even when the odds seemed stacked against you.

It's a story about the little guy who listens, beating the big company that long ago stopped listening.

It's a story about a powerful corporation moving to squash an upstart competitor and finding that in the end, our system works, and the laws are the same for the big and the small.

Those are good stories, the kind that sell books and movie tickets, because people love stories about how we can achieve our dreams, how hard work pays off, how our system still works, how a David can beat a Goliath.

But those aren't the only stories of our twenty years outside Fenway Park. What I lost sight of was that even though I own the magazine, it belongs to all the people who have made it a part of their lives. And those guys wrote back to me saying that their story, the story of how my magazine changed their lives, wasn't in my book at all.

Their story is about working at Fenway Park — the crowds, the excitement. Their story is about raking in money so fast they don't have time to stuff it into their apron.

Their story is about working all day at their regular job, then taking a bus and a train to get to the ballpark, even though the forecast is for rain.

Their story is about working every day of a 13-game homestand, losing their voice after eleven games, and going out there on the last day anyway and selling 300 programs and taking home a nice bonus.

Their story is about the camaraderie of working with the same guys, rain and shine, April through September, yelling at each other and laughing at each other and going out to eat afterwards.

Their story is about having the phone ring and having their friends say they saw them on FOX or ESPN. Their story is about going on the road to watch the Red Sox and having people walk up to them and say, "I know you! You sell magazines at Fenway!"

"The 15 years I've been involved with *Boston Baseball* have been very special, and I want to show my kids someday what I was a apart of," wrote one hawker. "I'm 32 years old, I'm not getting any younger. I want to be proud of something. I want to be able to take this book off my bookshelf any time and just read."

"I have to say that the *Boston Baseball* taught me a lot of stuff," wrote another. "How to have confidence, how to fight for my beliefs, how to stand up for myself, how to deal with people how to handle bad situations and whole of other things. Most of all, *Boston Baseball* gave me family!

"[But] I want to see more personal stories about the hawkers added into this... I believe *Boston Baseball* isn't *Boston Baseball* without the stories of the boys in it...

"Most of our stories have little to do with the development of the company, but it will show your readers that this company was more than just a business. There were some sad and wonderful parts in this company's life."

I had to admit that the hawkers were right. I took their advice and reworked parts of the book. While there's more to the magazine than the ballpark sales crew, I had to concede that working at the ballpark is the most dramatic and interesting part of the business.

Finally, I decided that I had neither the time or the talent to tell their stories; they were going to have to tell their stories themselves. And so as the 2009 season began, I postponed the publication of the book in order to include interviews with some of the veteran hawkers.

As that hawker said, we're not getting any younger, and I want to do this right. Because it's not just about me, it's about all the people who gave their time and energy to making *Boston Baseball* the critical and popular success that it is.

My commute takes me down from the North Shore these days. I cross the Tobin, get on Storrow Drive, exit at Kenmore, and then sneak down Newbury Street.

It's when I turn onto Newbury that I get my first glimpse of Fenway Park, the back of the bleachers and of the Green Monster, with the low-rise night clubs in the foreground and the light standards rising above.

At the end of Newbury I make a left onto Brookline Ave. There's a knot of scalpers on the corner already, four hours before game time.

I cross the bridge over the Mass Pike, shift into neutral, and coast down the street. I look for anything — unlicensed vendors, street musicians, hawkers for the *Globe* or *Herald* — that will impact business.

On Lansdowne Street, the sausage vendors are setting up. A line is forming at Game On, and across the street at the Beer Works. I glance down Yawkey Way as I roll past. Nick Jacobs is setting up his peanut cart.

I skirt the Twins Souvenirs loading dock, where a UPS truck, halfway up on the curb, is blocking traffic. Then I go left down an alley and into the VIP parking lot.

It's not a garden spot, this paved lot behind Brookline Ave. Half the lot is taken up by an old garage, gutted to fit more cars. That's where I work, in a cleared-out corner of that garage, but first I have to put my car someplace. The guys who work for the lot, Andre or Ducky, find a spot for me so that when I'm ready to leave at eight o'clock, five hours from now, we won't have to move too many cars.

I have everything I need for the day: change for the hawkers, my clipboard with the daily sales sheets, the month's sales figures ("the standings") and the gate assignments for the homestand. I might also have a box of red t-shirts and aprons, if they've gone home to be washed.

I'm rarely the first one at the park. Today there are three guys already there: Lemon, John Freeman, and our crazy Russian runner, Ilya.

Lemon is standing at the long plywood counter we cobbled together out of discarded building materials, stuffing stat inserts into magazines. He is *fast*. I'm not slow, but I can't touch Lemon. He regularly stuffs 15 boxes of magazines in an hour; that's 1800 magazines.

On his way to ballpark today, Lemon stopped at the Staples in the old Sears Building — now the Landmark Center — and picked up the inserts. These are letter-sized copies which we print each time a new team visits Fenway, with updated statistics for both the Red Sox and the visiting team. It's a popular feature but it's a real chore stuffing them into the magazines.

I'm delighted that Lemon is here, because otherwise I'd have to stuff the books myself, and get here a lot earlier to do it. Sometimes Lemon goes off and travels the world, flying no-name airlines and staying in hostels. When he returns he brings me coins from the places he has visited. Lemon has been working for me for 15 years.

John Freeman is here too. John is an old hippie with a southern drawl who has been working for me for seven years now. He is our oldest hawker, but he is still one of the best, although not so limber as he was a few years ago. He likes to get here early. John does not do things fast. He watches Lemon's hands slicing and dicing the magazines.

Ilya is occupied with the dolly, carrying boxes of magazines out of our storage closet and out to where Lemon can reach them. Ilya was born in Russia but raised here by his grandparents. He lives right around the corner from the ballpark. He would like to do things fast, like Lemon, but life is a second language to Ilya. Although he means well, he tends to get tangled up in his own underwear.

Over the next hour we'll get ready to sell magazines. Lemon, with his fast hands, will produce 15 stuffed boxes of magazines, 120 to a box, for a total of 1800 magazines. That should be enough for a weeknight, and I can always stuff another box or two if we're busier than expected. I post the hawker standings on our bulletin board so that the guys can check them as they come in, but I don't post the gate assignments.

Gate assignments are the most contentious part of the job. In order to get good coverage all around the ballpark, and not have the guys fight over the most lucrative areas, we have assigned names to different spots around the ballpark:

The Bridge
Gate A
Gate B
Gate C
Gate D
Gate E
The Ticket Office

John Freeman selling outside the Cask

The Diner
The Cask
The Parking Lot

"The Bridge" is the bridge over the Mass Pike from Kenmore Square. The hawker stationed there is the first hawker people will see, and everyone who uses the bridge has to pass within a few feet of our hawker. As a result, this is one of the best places to be assigned. When our all-times sales record gets broken, it's always by someone at the bridge.

We've had days when the guy at the bridge was so busy he didn't have time to put his money in his apron. I remember hawkers coming back with boxes emptied of magazines and filled up with crumpled bills. John Clougherty went up to the bridge one day and sold 962 magazines in two hours — eight magazines every minute.

The Cask, outside the entrance to the venerable Cask & Flagon, is about seventy yards behind the Bridge. Again, a lot of people walk past and they're all close enough to touch, so this is another good spot; you just stand there and let the crowd flow around you.

Gate A, right out in front of the turnstiles on Yawkey Way, is a great spot. So are the Ticket Office, on the corner of Brookline Ave and Yawkey Way in front of the Red Sox ticket office, and the Diner, which is the opposite corner, in front of what is now another Twins Souvenir location but which used to be the Fenway Diner.

On days when we expect to be busy, we might put two hawkers at Gate A and two at Gate D, which is outside the turnstiles at the opposite end of Yawkey Way. This is one of the ways we've compensated for the fact that since 2002, the City has allowed the Red Sox to close down Yawkey Way on game days, essentially turning that block of the street into their private property.

Our hawkers, who used to have the run of the street, are now restricted to either end of the street outside the turnstiles. We're a little further from the action, so we have to work harder and throw more hawkers out there in order to sell what we used to before the closure.

All of these spots have well-established reputations, and although some hawkers may favor one spot over another for their own reasons, there is substantial agreement over which gates are best. Soon after I started hiring hawkers — as opposed to relying on my friends and roommates — I realized that I had to set up a rotation so that the same people wouldn't be going to the same gates all the time. This is more fair, provides a change of scenery, and also ensures that the new hawkers occasionally get a shot at a good gate to show what they can do and move up in the hawker hierarchy.

At *Boston Baseball*, seniority counts, but is not decisive; it's all about how many magazines you sell. As you move up in the standings, you get better gates, and you make more money. Since good gates equal good money, assigning the gates can be problematic. Guys who aren't getting the gates they think they deserve get angry.

I spend a lot of time working out the gate arrangements so as to be as fair as possible, but I can't please everyone. As much time as I lavish on making out fair assignments, plans change, people don't show up, and stuff happens. It rains, for example. You can't sell magazines in the rain. We had a kid named Tim Michaud, and it seemed every time he was assigned to the bridge, his big day, it would rain. More about Tim later.

I make up the gate assignments in advance. I print them out and bring them in with me, but I keep them on my clipboard. As guys show up, I circle their names. When people don't show up, I have to switch people around to get the best coverage. I try to be fair, but we're all there to make money. Some of the hawkers try to peek at my clipboard as we're getting ready to sell. The veterans have a pretty good idea where they're going, but they never know for sure.

As the guys come in they'll stow their street clothes and their backpacks and put on their red *Boston Baseball* t-shirts. They'll put on an apron and fill one of the pockets with the free pencils we give away. Lemon and Ilya are counting the magazines into stacks of 20; most hawkers will take 40 or 60 magazines with them when they start selling. After that, Ilya circles the ballpark with several boxes of magazines on the dolly, keeping everyone supplied with magazines and change.

The goal is that nobody has to come all the way back to the garage to get more magazines, but it happens. When it does, the hawkers can be pretty rough with the runner if they think he's been slacking off. By letting someone run out of magazines, he's cost everyone money, because we're all working on commission — the hawker the runner, and myself.

At some point Sly comes in. At this point, the whole atmosphere changes, because Sly is a high-impact personality. Love or hate him, you know he's there.

Sly is the Man. He's our top seller. He started working for me as a skinny teenager back in 1992. He walked up to me on Yawkey Way wearing a Giants shirt, #22, for his hero, Will Clark, and asked for a job selling magazines. He claims I brushed him off at first because we had a full crew, but eventually he got a chance and he quickly established himself as one of the top guys.

Sly checks the standings, not to see where he is, because he knows damn well that he's in first place, but to see how far ahead he is. He then taunts the second- and third-place guys. If he's in a good mood he probably has an entertaining story to tell about last night's game, *Star Wars* action figures, his adventures at his other jobs, or his time in the Marine Corps, but often he is pissed off about something and then it's best to

The hawkers are supplied with $2 buttons. Some hawkers decorate themselves with five or six

avoid him, because if he's pissed off about something, it can easily turn into him being pissed at anyone who gets in his way.

Sly is a tremendous hawker, the best we've ever had, and he's hugely popular with the customers, who only have to deal with him for ten seconds at a stretch. He's full of energy and conviction, and he's always coming up with ideas about how to sell more magazines. But he can also be a pain in the ass. He constantly reminds us all how many magazines he has sold. He loves to tell me his sales have paid for my house, my boat, my children's college educations. There's some truth to this, because he has sold an *enormous* number of magazines. But we do get tired of hearing it.

Sylvester "Sly" Egidio

*Boston Baseball* wouldn't be the same without Sly, but I think the other hawkers would rejoice. It would be quieter, calmer. Someone else would have a chance to win the sales contests. But we wouldn't sell as many magazines, that's for sure.

For an evening game, 7:05 nowadays, we start by sending out the hawker assigned to Gate A. He gets a seven-minute head start; an opportunity to work the crowd that is gathering in front of the turnstiles before the ballpark opens. On a good day, this can mean 40-60 extra sales. Then I hand thirty one-dollar bills to each of the other hawkers (some have also brought their own change) as I read off their gate assignments and they walk or run, as the case may be, to their gates.

Ilya and I are left alone to load up the dolly with three or four boxes of magazines. He also gets some ones, in case anyone runs short of change, as well as some signs for the hawkers at the Bridge and the Cask: "PROGRAMS $2". He will immediately bring a box up to the guys at the Bridge and the Cask, then begin circling the ballpark, keeping everyone supplied.

Once Ilya is gone, I am left with a mess to clean up. There are empty boxes scattered around with their flaps ripped off. The hawkers put the flaps on their forearms and then stack the books on top, for a more stable platform and also, on warm days, to keep from sweating on the magazines. The boxes get broken down and stacked for recycling, the stray pencils get picked up off the floor, and the roster gets readjusted to reflect who ended up going where.

I fill out a daily sheet that tracks how many magazines each hawker left with and how many Ilya has taken out. Ilya has a matching clipboard, and every time he gives magazines to a hawker, he makes a note. At the end of the day he'll bring his clipboard back and presumably his totals will match what he has taken out, minus whatever he brings back. If the numbers don't match, we have to try and figure out what happened before the hawkers come back in.

But that's two hours away. Once our corner of the garage is neatened up and the daily sheet is filled out, I have an opportunity to walk around the ballpark and see how things are going.

By the time I get out there, the gates are open. The crowd that gathered in front of the turnstiles, waiting to get in, has gone into the park and for the next half hour it will be pretty slow. Then the crowds will gradually increase until the flow peaks in the last twenty minutes before game time.

I make a circuit of the park, checking in with each hawker. I ask them how it's going, how the crowd is. It's true that the hawkers only work for two and half hours, but for those two and half hours, they're going non-stop, all out. Yelling and selling! It takes an enormous amount of energy. By the end of a long homestand, even the veterans start to lose their voices.

I walk over to Nick Jacobs and pick up a fistful of salted peanuts.

Nick bags all the peanuts in the hours before the game and now he shuffles the bags forward to the front of the cart like a store clerk facing shelves. All the season ticketholders know Nick. Some of them have known Nick since he was a kid and worked here with his father.

Over the years, I've seen Nick's cart help come and go. There was a kid named Jamie who used to hang a cracked peanut shell from the lobe of his ear like an earring. We

Nick Jacobs

Lemon as Darth Vader

thought that was pretty funny, but he and Nick had a falling out. Then Nick's brother worked with him for a while. He was a little nuts. Nick himself is a great guy, very humble.

I eat a few peanuts and we might talk for a minute, but only for a minute — we both have work to do. I continue around the park. Some of the guys I look for are Pat and Brian, who work the Twins Souvenir carts; the Sausage King, whose cart is now up on Lansdowne Street by Gate E; George, another sausage vendor; and Keith Durham, who sells 'Hats, Caps, T-shirts, All Sizes!" on Lansdowne. Keith is assisted by Tim Dineen, who sold magazines for me for many years.

Down by Gate C is Ken Melanson, who sells baseball cards and other items, and then back at Gate D there's Jim Parry, who sells sunglasses and "pop-up um-ba-rellas" on rainy days. I've been working at Fenway 20 years now, but all these guys have been here longer than me. I'm the new kid, 44 years old and with 20 years at the park.

Maybe that's one of the reasons I wasn't able to pull all these guys together a few years ago to resist the Red Sox' takeover of Yawkey Way, where most of them had lucrative locations before 2002. With the exception of Nick, I'll bet not one of them is making what they made six years ago, unless by raising prices.

Back at the garage I'll check the number of boxes to see if Ilya has been back for more; very likely he has. I'll note the number on my clipboard, and then if my cellphone isn't ringing and no magazines need to be stuffed and everything seems to be running smoothly, I'll go grab a bite to eat.

Later, in the last half hour before the game starts, everything starts to happen faster. Ilya's trips to the garage for more boxes become more frequent. He runs in, sweating, loads up the dolly, and runs out. If we have time we'll attempt to balance our accounts. He has a tendency to waste time and energy running errands for the hawkers — bringing them drinks or fetching them items from their backpacks. I try to keep him focused on the job. He's getting better, but he's not very efficient yet.

Lemon, of the fast hands, was an excellent runner for many years. But when he finished growing he was 6-1 — being tall is a big help when you're hawking in a crowd — and he discovered there was more money to be made hawking than running. Hawking also gives him an outlet for his creative side. For big games, he likes to paint his body various colors (usually red) or with various mottos ("Cowboy Up!") or dress in costume.

A few years ago, after Larry Lucchino made his "Evil Empire" comment about the Yankees, Lemon bought a Darth Vader costume, painted it red, and put a Red Sox "B" on the front of the helmet. He looked great, and he was all over TV, but he had a hard time selling magazines in that getup.

Out Ilya goes again, making a last trip up to Gate A, where the late action is. I have the radio on now, listening to the pregame show. The national anthem will play, the game will start, and the first inning will be well underway before the first hawkers return. The crowds tend to die off first at the back side of the ballpark, at gates B and D. Gate A will stay busy a little longer. The hawkers come in, drop their returns, and give me their two cents.

"What a great crowd!" or "Mike, it sucked out there tonight." or "I started off great, and then it died." or "It was dead and then everyone came in the last half-hour!"

John Freeman, who is more scientific than most, gives me his breakdown. "Mike, I sold a hundred the first hour and a hundred and forty after that."

In recent years, with the tickets having gotten so much more expensive, the crowds have changed, and not for the better. The hawkers often are very negative about the people they saw: "There weren't any real fans tonight." or "I've never seen so many clueless people."

It used to be we saw the same people again and again over the course of the season. People would walk up to you and they'd have the money already in their hand. They knew what they wanted and where they were going. Now it seems like every night it's a new bunch of people, most of whom seem to come to one game a year, if that.

They're asking for directions. They're fumbling in their wallet. They're milling around in front of the turnstiles, looking lost, or talking on their cell phones.

When Ilya and I add our clipboards together we know how many magazines each hawker has taken. Counting their returns, we figure out how much money they should be turning in. The counting takes a while, though, and there is always a lot of banter, with the game on in the background.

Sometimes there are arguments. When hawkers wander into each other's territory, there can be problems, and that has to be settled. Sometimes the hawkers confront each other directly; other times, they'll wait until the offender is out of earshot, or gone for the day, before complaining to me.

The worst part of the job is when the money doesn't work out. This can happen for any number of reasons. Theft is the obvious one, and it does happen, but the runner can make mistakes, the hawker can give incorrect change or flat-out lose money, and of course we can make mistakes in our math or in our counting.

This isn't a casino and we don't do strip searches; we make an effort to figure out where we might have gone wrong before we start pointing fingers. Sometimes the money appears, stuffed into the wrong pocket, into a corner of an apron, or a twenty is tucked in with some tens; sometimes the returns were wrong, or hawkers left with more or less magazines than we had them written down for. Sometimes the runner, in his haste, puts 20 magazines into Ryan's column when those magazines really went to Joe.

Usually we figure it out. Sometimes we can't. If I'm really stumped it comes down to the reputation of the hawker. I might let it go, I might offer to split the missing sum, or I might take it all out of the hawker's pay.

Most of my hawkers are guys who have been working for me for several years. I know them and they know me. They know I'm not going to cheat them. They also know I am not going to rip their head off for a sum that amounts to bus fare0. And some of the guys who have been around a while know the system well enough to know where the cracks are. Those guys might get a peek at my clipboard, and if a mistake has been made in their favor, they know they can pocket the money and nobody will ever be the wiser.

It's the worst part of the job, having money go missing, not being able to figure out where it went, and to have make a judgment that may or may not end up being fair.

If it's bad, my wife can always tell when I get home from the ball park. She can see it in my face. And she gets madder than I do about it. Not about the money, but the idea that the hawkers might be stealing from me.

Most days it all works out, and as we count out the hawkers, they are paid in cash and their focus shifts to their plans for the evening. They've got money in their pockets and it's not even 8 PM. Some years the hawkers have all hung out together, gone out together, gone into the game, but there's less of that now. So they get paid, get back into their street clothes, and head out.

Ilya and I organize the returns, repack the boxes, put the magazines back into storage, and prepare the money to be deposited. When everyone has counted out I add up the totals for the day and pay the runner a percentage of the sales. I'll also pay Lemon for stuffing the boxes earlier. We'll neaten up our space, turn off the radio, and call it a day.

Back in my car, heading up to the North Shore, I have the game on the radio. Hopefully, the Red Sox are winning.

# Back Story

After twenty years, I can do this job in my sleep. Sometimes I do. But we've come a long way. It wasn't like this back in 1990, when I got the idea to publish my own baseball newsletter and sell it outside Fenway Park.

I had grown up a Red Sox fan. My father was born in 1934 and he grew up with Ted Williams, Bobby Doerr, and Johnny Pesky. His parents were Red Sox fans as well.

His father was a liquor salesman — both inside and outside of Prohibition — which was the perfect calling card for the hard-drinking Red Sox front office. In fact, he and my father were able to get into the Red Sox clubhouse after one of the games of the 1946 World Series. Unfortunately, it was a game that the Red Sox lost, and the players were not in the best of moods.

My father's sister married a Braves fan, but she herself was true to the Red Sox, and owned terrific season tickets two rows up from first base, a section or two beyond the dugout. I remember going with her to Game Seven of the 1975 World Series. After the game ended, I hopped over the wall onto the field and gathered a handful of dirt from first base, where my hero Carl Yastrzemski played then.

I had been born in Boston and attended my first game when I was five. I have only the vaguest recollection of being surrounded by Big People and of the electronic scoreboard winking strange numbers at me. Then we moved to California, but I remained loyal to Boston. Growing up in Goleta, ninety minutes north of Los Angeles, I was a Red Sox and Patriots fan. My father took me to the Big A to root for visiting Boston against the hometown Angels; many times to Chavez Ravine to see the Dodgers; and to the Coliseum to watch USC and Notre Dame. I rooted for the Fighting Irish, because Yaz had gone there.

When my friends and I rode our bikes to the 7-11, I was hoping to get my slurpee in the Carl Yastrzemski cup. When we bought baseball cards, I traded my Dodgers for Red Sox. One day an older kid in the neighborhood gave me a card from 1968, a World Series highlight card that showed Yastrzemski bashing one of his two home runs against the Cardinals in Game Two. This became my prize possession.

Moving back to Sudbury, Massachusetts after six years in California,

I resumed my love affair with the Red Sox. A close friend of the family, Howard Abel, lived one town over in Wayland, and once when we were at his home he played his "Impossible Dream" album for me, with Ken Coleman's epic narration of the 1967 season.

I was thunderstruck, and it must have been obvious, because he gave me the record and I still have it today. I played that record until I had it memorized, I knew just where to plunk the needle down to get the highlight I wanted: "Yastrzemski's going hard, way back, way back... and he dives and makes a TERRIFIC CATCH! One of the best catches you'll ever see by Yastrzemski in left field! He went back and came down with that ball!"

My next-door neighbor, Marc David, and I would act out the highlights in my room with the album playing, diving across the room, glove outstretched, to crash-land on the bed. Outside, we would play 500 and pitch to each other as the catcher ad-libbed a Red Sox-Yankees play-by-play.

Eventually I discovered girls, music, and beer, and baseball took a back seat. When I was a college freshman in 1983, my father called my dorm at the University of Pennsylvania and told me he had tickets to the last game of the season, the game that would mark Yastrzemski's retirement. I decided I'd rather stay in Philadelphia, where my girlfriend was scheduled to visit.

I did find my way back to baseball, though. My college friends were all baseball fans. Mike Marinari was a Phillies fan. Mark Broitman was a Mets fan — there were a lot of Mets fans at Penn. Kevin Lewis was a Yankee fan. Rodney Paul was an Orioles fan. We would ride SEPTA down to Veteran's Stadium to watch the Phillies.

The Vet — or the Day-Glo Toilet Bowl, as we called it — was an eye-opener after Fenway Park. The Phils were a good club when I arrived as a freshman, but went downhill as Mike Schmidt and Steve Carlton got older. I remember when Schmidt got hurt one year and Luis Aguayo took over at third; we adopted Luis and became his biggest boosters.

Anyhow, we'd go to the Vet and keep score until we were drunk, or else we would try to sneak into better seats on the lower levels. Getting drunk at the Vet was not hard. At Fenway in those days, there were no beer vendors in the stands. You had to leave your seat to go wait in line in the damp, smelly concourse to buy two flat Genesee Lights on draft. But at the Vet there were beer vendors who would, on command, crack

Penn, 1986: the author, catching, and Rodney Paul, batting

open an ice-cold 16-ounce can of Schmidt's and pour it right in front of your eyes. And this for a dollar less than in Boston!

At home for the summer, my friends and I would drive into Fenway for games; I remember parking right on Lansdowne Street. My friend Greg bought a Yankees cap he'd wear to the games, just to be obnoxious.

After Yaz retired, the team was not so interesting, but the 1984 Red Sox got me through a long summer of working the night shift as a security guard at the Raytheon plant in Wayland. Once the plant had closed and we'd checked everyone out and hung up all the badges, there wasn't much to do but go on rounds once an hour. We weren't allowed a radio in the guard shack, but sometimes the regular guards would let me sit in my car and listen to the games.

Marty Barrett was my favorite player in those days. I went to a game that summer and he was signing autographs down the left-field line, so I ran down and asked him to sign my program as "Marty Ballgame".

"Are you serious?" he asked.

"Absolutely," I replied. And he did.

After Penn I was accepted to the Iowa Writer's Workshop, in Iowa City. While out there I had a chance to go to games at Wrigley Field as well as County Stadium in Milwaukee and the old Comiskey Park in

Chicago, both gone now. I discovered Bill James and his wonderful *Baseball Abstract*. I start collecting baseball cards again — even worked my own table at the Wellfleet Flea Market during the summers — and joined a rotisserie league with my college buddies.

After two years I returned to Boston with a subsistence-level teaching job and a real desire, pent up over six years in Philadelphia and Iowa City, to be down at Fenway Park. I went to 20 or more games a year. I kept score. I never left early. In the summers I went to the batting cage and took BP at Little League fields. I played Strat-O-Matic and APBA. For my 21st birthday I received a Red Sox warmup jacket, a George Brett Rawlings glove, and a black 32-ounce bat.

At some point during the 1989 season it occurred to me that the official Red Sox scorebook/magazine left a great deal to be desired. First of all, the scorecard itself was terrible. In order to make room for beer advertisements (I believe it was Budweiser) the working area of the scorecards had been shrunk to half a page. It was on glossy paper, so pencils were of no avail; you had to use a pen, and if you made a mistake, forget it. And there was no space provided to track the pitchers.

Eventually I began bringing my own store-bought scorecard book to the games, but still I would have bought the Red Sox' magazine if only it had come out more often. It was changed just twice a year; there was an April/May edition, a June/July edition, and an August/September edition.

I also wanted to see some info about the visiting teams; reports on what was going on in the minor league organization, and up-to-date statistics, which back then were only printed in the *Globe* on Sundays, to accompany Peter Gammons' ground-breaking baseball reportage. Gammons, Nick Cafardo, and Bill James were my heroes. Whoever was putting together the Red Sox scorebook was not in their league.

Well, I got it into my head that the Red Sox could do better, and that I with my newly-minted master's degree from Iowa was the guy to help them do it. I wrote the Red Sox a letter outlining the shortcomings of their magazine and suggesting that they hire me to improve it for them.

Well, obviously things would have turned out a lot differently if the Sox had hired me. But they're the Red Sox, they get a lot of letters like that one, and mine ended up with all the rest. The difference, I guess, was that I decided not to accept that as the final answer.

At this time I was living with my college roommate, Kevin, and his girlfriend in Medford. I was teaching days at Bentley College in Waltham, and one night a week at Merrimack College in North Andover, and making about $22,000 a year. Kevin thought that was pretty funny. He was working for Raytheon and making twice that. There were no pretty coeds at Raytheon, however.

At Christmas my parents took my sister and I on a vacation to Cancun, and on the flight home I broached my idea to my father. I needed a desktop computer — newfangled and expensive things back then — along with a scanner and laser printer and some software, which altogether was going to cost several thousand dollars. That was a lot of money in 1990.

My father will admit that he never imagined this new business idea was going to go anywhere, but he did think that in the attempt I would teach myself some new skills and have some valuable experiences. So he loaned me the money, I bought the equipment, and I spent the winter learning to use my new Mac Plus and in particular the PageMaker software that I was going to use to design my newsletter, which I had decided to call *Baseball Underground*.

I started writing some of the articles, the ones that could be written ahead of time. I remember going down to the Boston Public Library and going through the microfilm of the Boston *Globe* from 1975, putting together stories and box scores on that pennant-winning season, which would celebrate its 15th anniversary that coming summer.

Nobody who is under 30 today can understand how frustrating it was, how completely futile it could feel, working with the early computers. Tasks that today take place instantaneously used to involve staring at ticking "watch" icons for entire minutes. Whenever you opened a file, resized a window, saved a file, whatever — it took *time*. And the time added up.

Then there were the crashes. Every time that little wristwatch started ticking, you had to wonder if the computer was going to crash, erasing everything you'd done since your last save.

Putting together a 12-page newsletter on my original set of equipment took three times as long as it takes me to put together an 88-page full-color magazine today. Never will I forget the long, late nights, the computer crashes after half an hour of watching the little watch go around, the trips to the corner store for Mountain Dew to help me stay awake. I worked long days and longer nights, peering at a monochrome screen that might have been eight inches wide.

It all seems like a long time ago — and it was. Jean Yawkey was still alive, and John Harrington was running the team for her. Lou Gorman was the General Manager. Joe Morgan was the manager, still riding the high of Morgan Magic two summers before. And the most expensive ticket in Fenway Park was $16.

# 1990

When Opening Day finally rolled around, delayed a few days by a month-long lockout earlier in the spring, I was ready with my first issue.

"Rookie Newsletter Steps Up to Plate" the front page declared, above a photo of Mike Greenwell.

It was twelve pages, black and white, on bright, white stock. Stapled into the middle was a scorecard of my own crude design on card stock. I had written every word of every article. There was one ad, for a baseball shop down on the Cape run by my friend Bill Muse.

The articles were straightforward. I had identified what I thought were the weaknesses in the official scorebook/magazine, and so from the very first issue, *Baseball Underground* featured objective reporting on the state of the team, an article on each of the visiting teams, and my clunky scorecard, as well as articles on baseball-card collecting (a red-hot hobby at the time) and rotisserie baseball, which was just taking off.

There was also my feature on the 1975 Red Sox, following that team through their historic season complete with box scores and standings.

I printed up 2500 copies and recruited Kevin and some other friends to help me hand them out, for free, in front of the ballpark.

My plan was to publish according to the Red Sox schedule. Rather than publish weekly or monthly, I would have new issues come out whenever the Red Sox came home to begin a series of games. If the Sox came home for three, left for three, and came home for three more, I'd group those two series together into one issue.

By studying the Sox' slate, I was able to put together a schedule that would include ten issues a season. That would give me a chance to make my money back on each issue while still coming out often enough to be timely. At that point, the official Red Sox magazine was only going through three editions a year, and I felt good about coming out three times as often.

The big day came. The second issue came off the presses, and I threw the bundles in the trunk of my 1983 Mustang convertible and set off for Kenmore Square. In those days I would get into town early and hunt for a spot near the gates, because I had to carry the newsletters up

The first issue

**Baseball Underground!**

| April 9, 1990 | Opening Day! | Volume 1, Number 1 |

## Rookie Newsletter Steps Up to Plate

Welcome to the first issue of Baseball Underground! Dedicated to the Boston baseball scene, Baseball Underground has been designed to inform and entertain you, the serious baseball fan. Each issue contains:

- ❑ **Profiles of the Visiting Teams**
- ❑ **Minor League and Amateur Reports**
- ❑ **Card Collecting & Rotisserie Tips**
- ❑ **User-Friendly Scorecard**

not to mention a Coaches' Box that taps the experience and knowledge of local college coaches, a look back at the heart-stopping 1975 season, and essays, statistics, & analyses you will find nowhere else. You've had enough of stale features, sycophantic reporting, and cramped scorecards—we're here to offer you a choice. Baseball Underground intends to be your complete resource for Boston baseball!

With a new issue for each Red Sox homestand, Baseball Underground is available outside Fenway Park before every home game, as well as through subscription and at selected baseball card stores and shows.

### BoSox Open the 1990 Season against Detroit, Milwaukee

Baseball at last—cause for rejoicing! But will the schedule shuffling that resulted from the month-long lockout help or hurt the Red Sox?

The original schedule called for the Sox to begin with nine games against the American League's two last place clubs, Detroit and Chicago. Now, the Red Sox will open here against the Tigers (see Page 2) and then face the dangerous Brewers (see Page 3) seven times in nine days.

The Red Sox have historically bested the Brewers (161-136) and have dominated them in Fenway (90-57). But Milwaukee took last year's season series, 7-6, and the Red Sox don't often play well in County Stadium.

One thing that should favor the Red Sox is their 12-8 lifetime record against Milwaukee's top three starters, Higuera, Bosio, and Navarro.

Since Milwaukee's talent in this weak division makes them legitimate contenders, every win against them will be twice as sweet. The Red Sox would like to establish an edge in these early games against the Brewers, who they won't see again until late in July.

The next Red Sox homestand commences on April 24. Look for the second issue of Baseball Underground before the games against California, Oakland, and Seattle! Read and enjoy!

*Mike Greenwell leads the Sox against the Tigers and Brewers in the first homestand of the season.*

**Inside:**

- ❑ **Tigers, Brewers In Depth**
- ❑ **Beware those Brewer Prospects**
- ❑ **Tony Conigliaro Remembered**
- ❑ **Opening Day 1975**
- ❑ **Best Buys in BoSox Rookie Cards**
- ❑ **Ballpark Effects & the Smart Rotisserie Owner**

the street to where we were selling. Days when my teaching job didn't allow me to get the park early enough to find a good spot, I might have to trudge a fair distance with a heavy box of magazines and all my other paraphernalia (aprons, buttons, etc.) on my shoulder.

The day that the second issue debuted — my first day actually *selling* my newsletter — I took in $68. I don't remember whether I was ecstatic or disappointed, but it didn't matter. I had ordered a lot of newsletters, and I needed to pay that printing bill. I was out there the next day, and the next day, and the next.

And it took off! For that second issue, we averaged 150 sales per game.

One of the best things about being there on the sidewalk, selling the newsletter every day, was that people could tell darn well that I was not just the guy selling the newsletter but also the editor, publisher, writer, designer, and everything else. And they weren't shy with their comments.

Those early readers in the spring and summer of 1990 gave me a lot of good advice, and I took it.

Every issue, we sold more copies. By the third issue I was able to add minor league coverage, including reports from Brian Mullen, who was on the spot in Winter Haven. The readers asked for rosters, and I complied. And we picked up a few advertisers, mostly Kenmore Square businesses such as the Pizza Pad, which was located on the corner where the Store 24 is now, and Whippersnappers, down at the tip of the triangle of Brookline & Boylston, where D'Angelos is now.

Most importantly, I found a home away from home. No more trudging up and down the street with boxes on my shoulder! The Batter's Box, a step-down eatery on the corner of the Brookline & Yawkey, right across from the Red Sox ticket office, offered us the space under a couple of stools at the end of their counter. We'd leave the box of magazines there, and run in from the street to grab more when we ran out.

Barry was the owner of the Batter's Box. He and his family were nice folks, and the place was an absolute bedlam on game days. I'm sure it cost them money to reserve that space for us, but we did eat there 81

The author,
June, 1990

times a year. We were loyal!

By the end of July I had doubled the size of the newsletter, from 12 to 24 pages, and switched to a lighter paper stock to keep my costs down. I was offering subscriptions ($8.50 for ten issues). And I'd added instructions on how to score the games, as well as a map of the ballpark, as a result of reader feedback.

Now we were selling 600 copies a game! I had everyone I knew down at the park selling the newsletter — my father, my sister, my friends, girlfriend, coworkers, contributors. It was amazing, selling that many books, more than I'd ever imagined we would sell. I wasn't prepared for the feeling I got from coming up with an idea, making a product with own hands, as it were, and watching people snap it up like hotcakes.

After the games I'd go back to the apartment in Medford and dump out the money and count it all, and it was exhilarating. I couldn't wait to get back to the ballpark for the next game, to start work on the next issue, to come up with new ideas that would make *Baseball Underground* bigger and better.

In August, I added complete AL and NL pitching rosters so fans could follow the out-of-town scoreboard in left field. We also began a "Trivia Challenge" sponsored by Rodman Insurance, a firm that not coincidentally had a close family friend as a partner. We had fun coming up with the trivia questions at family gatherings.

By the fall I had a sense that this was the start of something. I continued to flesh out the newsletter with suggestions from readers and contributors and with ideas of my own. By the end of the year we had replaced that first lame scorecard with a full four-page insert that was better organized and had plenty of room for anything you might want to keep track of.

I moved to Somerville in September, just as the Red Sox were staking their place in the playoffs, with my high school friend Greg. We lived just outside of Davis Square — before it became trendy — down the street from the fabulous Redbone's BBQ.

It had been a pretty good season for the Red Sox. As long as they had Roger Clemens they had a pretty good pitching staff — excellent, by Red Sox standards — but the offense was in decline. The Sox led the league in batting average and OBP, but they had very little power. They finished first in a weak division, winning 88 games and edging out Toronto. That earned them the right to be swept by the A's in the playoffs, a series memorable only for the incident in which Roger Clemens was tossed by Gerry Cooney.

I continued teaching at Bentley and at Merrimack, but still found time put out a small Winter Meetings issue in December. I mailed it to my handful of subscribers and gave it out at baseball card shows. I agitated for Tom Brunansky to be let go and Mike Boddicker re-signed, but the Red Sox did the reverse, and then went out and signed Matt Young, Danny Darwin, and Jack Clark.

I had mixed feelings about the signings and about the news from the farm system, which was barren. In truth, as excited as I was about the Red Sox and about my new business, the state of the team was worrisome.

Shelly Rutstein, in the alley behind Mom & Pop's Pizza

When March rolled around, I was out again with a small Spring Training issue, and I made the first of a series of spring trips to Winter Haven to collect stories and photos that I could use as the season went along.

When I had started *Baseball Underground*, I never imagined that I would able to get media credentials from the Red Sox and cover the team the way the professionals did. Just one year in, I now had a feeling that while we might reach enough people to qualify for credentials, we had started down a path that would make us competitors rather than partners with the Red Sox.

Throughout our first year of publication, I had positioned *Baseball Underground* as an alternative to the official magazine, a product which had several glaring weaknesses. It was premature for me to imagine that my product was, overall, better than theirs. But it did have a number of features that appealed to people. The fact that by the end of our first year we could sell several hundred copies on any given day was a sign that we'd struck a chord with many fans.

I had no contact with the Red Sox during the first year of publication, other than to write them a letter in December of 1990 requesting media credentials for 1991. I got back a terse letter from Mary Jane Ryan, Coordinator of Credentials, stating that "If your publications is [sic] available at local newsstands" we would be eligible for credentials on a limited basis.

I had no plans at that time for newsstand distribution, so I filed the letter away, and that had been the extent of our communication when I arrived in Florida in March. Summoning all my courage, I presented myself at the trailer occupied by the Red Sox' public relations staff and was waved in to see Jim Samia, an assistant to longtime Red Sox PR chief Dick Bresciani.

Jim asked me what I wanted. I told him I published a newsletter about the team and was looking for credentials. Jim looked up at me and said, in a withering tone, "You're the kid who says his scorecard is better than ours."

I said yes, that was me.

Jim glanced down at the papers on his desk.

"I don't think we can help you," he said, and that was that.

Still, he hadn't asked security to remove me from the premises — I don't think there *was* any security back in those days — and there was nobody to stop me from walking over to the minor league complex, so interviewed a couple of minor leaguers, snapped photos of a B game that was going on, and began my career as a media guerrilla.

Accepting the fact that I wasn't going to get credentials from the team, I soon figured out how to get the material I needed. Each spring I would book a room at the cheapest hotel I could find, preferably the one where the team's minor league players were staying. I would rent the cheapest sub-compact I could find. Instead of eating in restaurants, I would hit the Winn-Dixie the day I got off the plane, load up on peanut butter, bread, milk, Cheerios, and beer, and buy a big styrofoam cooler to keep it all in.

Back in my motel room, I'd punch holes in the bottom of the cooler so it could drain. Then I'd put in the bathtub and fill it up with my groceries and ice from the ice machine in the lobby. Instant refrigerator!

Days when the Red Sox were home, I would be one of the first people through the turnstile. Buying the best ticket available — spring training tickets probably averaged $5 then — I would go straight down to the field, near the batting circle, get the sun over my shoulder, and take photos from that vantage point throughout batting practice and fielding practice, until the rightful owners of the seats showed up.

Sometimes my own seats were good enough to continue to shoot from, sometimes not, but at any rate I usually went though several rolls of film. That first spring training I was shooting with a Pentax SLR I borrowed from my sister Robin.

After the game, if there were nothing going on at the back fields, I would head over to Eckerd Drug and drop off my film. Over the course of my two-week stay the folks at Eckerd would get used to me and my request that the photos be developed light, please, because at home I'd have to scan them and it was better to start with a light original. If Eckerd had a special or a coupon going, I was sure to take advantage of it.

One year Eckerd had a special where you only had to pay for the prints you wanted. Since my policy was always to shoot, shoot, shoot, hoping only to get three or four keepers per 35-picture roll, this was a godsend. The framers of that offer had never envisioned someone like me, who would bring in eight or ten rolls every day, keep just a few photos per roll, and return the rest! I'm surprised they didn't roll down the metal gates when they saw me pull into the parking lot.

My equipment wasn't good, my skills weren't good, and most of my early photos were useless. However, I did occasionally take a winner, a shot that I'd use later on in the season, maybe even one that was good enough to be a cover. And in taking all these photos, I met up with fans who were doing the same thing, for fun mostly, and I also met Tyler Bolden.

Tyler was what you might call semi-pro, a self-employed landscaper from Lake Alfred, not far from Winter Haven, who liked to go down to the ballpark and take pictures. He was good at it, had decent equipment, and he had made friends with the players and front office of the Red Sox by giving prints to anyone who asked nicely.

Tyler always had a couple of minor leaguers who he had become especially friendly with, and he'd send me terrific pictures of them, but while Tyler was a good photographer, he wasn't much of a talent scout. I don't think any of his buddies ever made it out of Double-A.

When I met Tyler, he had contributed a few photos to team publications such as *DieHard*, a Red Sox newsletter that had started publishing in the 1980s and was sold mostly through subscription. He had also done some work for *Baseball America*, which was a bigger deal.

Covering the team from the outside looking in could be a lonely experience. Once or twice I had a friend join me for a week in Florida, but most of the time I was there by myself, making the long drives by myself, watching batting practice by myself, eating peanut butter sandwiches in my hotel room by myself.

A better salesperson would have taken advantage of the many chances to make friends and sell subscriptions to all the Red Sox fans who surrounded me at the games, watching BP, at the hotel pool. But I wasn't interested in chatting up the folks in the seats next to me. I was interested in getting an interview down at the minor league fields before the game. I was interested in getting a usable photo of Jack Clark, of Danny Darwin, of Phil Plantier.

Tyler was a big help to me, not only because he gave me tips on how to take better photos, but because he gave me someone to hang out with. Tyler was a lot of fun. Although a good ten years older than me, he had a youthful outlook and a great sense of humor. We would carpool to the away games, go out for lunch and dinner, and soon he was bringing me home to meet his wife and family. Tyler could fill up a long car ride with wide-ranging discussions of antiques, photography, the Beatles, and his experiences as a landscaper and in the Marine Corps.

Tyler's photos soon became a staple in *Baseball Underground*, and for several years I paid Tyler a flat fee per issue — I forget what it was, but it wasn't much — and he sent me anything he thought I might be able to use. As a result, the quality of our photography made a giant leap forward beginning in 1991. Tyler also introduced me to other photographers such as Steve Moore and Morris Fostoff, whose work would appear in *Baseball Underground* and *Boston Baseball* for many years to come.

It wasn't just the photography that helped *Baseball Underground* make a great leap forward in 1991. I added spot color to the magazine. At first I added red, but the screens (shaded areas) came out pink, so I tried blue, then red and blue. By June I had it figured out — red *and* blue, with black for the text and photos. The overall look was livelier, although the photo reproduction wasn't great. We went back to a heavier stock, and since the page count was now up to 32, the newsletter had some heft to it.

I added new features in 1991 as well: local and amateur baseball

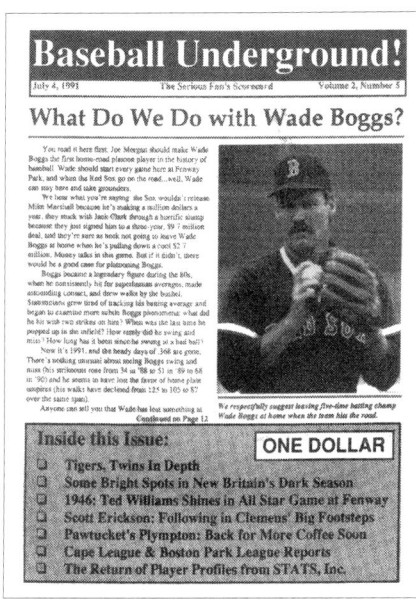

July, 1991

coverage, including the local college scene and the Boston Park League, and a National League column, which was initially written by my college friend Rodney Paul.

Rodney and I had met in my last year at Penn. He was a year ahead of me, but he still had some work to do to finish his degree. Rodney used to take SEPTA down to the Vet with us to watch the Phillies. Rodney liked to keep score, although he was easily distracted, and his scorecards were sprinkled with notations of "WW" — "Wasn't Watching".

Rodney used his own scorecards, which he brought to the ballpark mounted on a clipboard. Somehow I ended up with his clipboard and we are still using it today at Fenway Park. Although most of it is covered with various stickers (for baseball teams, radio stations, political candidates, and environmental groups), Rodney's name and Philadelphia phone number from 25 years ago can still be made out.

Rodney lived off campus, grew his own peppers and made terrific chili. He was from Delaware and thus, an Orioles fan. At our college graduation in front of ten thousand people at Franklin Field, we were handed cards to fill out so that we could have our names read correctly as we collected our diplomas. Worried that the speaker would mispronounce my name, I wrote it out phonetically: Michael RUTTSTEEN.

The speaker pronounced my last name correctly, but said "Michelle" instead of "Michael".

Rodney, sitting next to me, wrote out "Rodney Brooks Robinson Paul". The speaker evidently thought that four names were too many, and read them as two separate individuals. "Rodney Brooks" she intoned, followed by "Robinson Paul."

To this day, there are members of Rodney's family who don't believe he ever graduated.

Rodney moved to San Francisco after graduation and adopted the Giants. He was a big fan of Larry King, and would periodically send me cassette tapes made up of corny baseball songs and excerpts from King's radio show relating to baseball. Rodney himself appeared a couple of times on the show.

As a caller, he sang his "Chinese Food at the Baseball Game" Song:

*Take me out to the ballgame,*
*Take me out with the crowd!*
*Buy me some chow mein and beef szechuan,*

*I don't care if my egg roll gets cold!*

*Oh, it's root, root, root for the Phillies,*
*If our fortune's no good it's a shame!*
*For it's one, two, three bowls of rice*
*At the old ballgame!*

Larry praised the "ingenuity" of that song, prompting Rodney to show up at a live broadcast in San Francisco a few years later — "and here's a young man with an Orioles cap and a Giants shirt, and that intrigues me..."

Rodney would later become a world traveler and a dedicated diabetes fundraiser through the Napa Valley 'Tour de Cure', but in his salad days in the Bay Area he wrote engagingly about the National League for *Baseball Underground*.

Another writer we added for our second season was Fred C. Harris, who had written a neat little book called *The Great American Baseball Card Flipping, Trading, and Bubble Gum Book* in the 1970s, and operated The Great American Baseball Card Store in Concord, Massachusetts.

I had loved Fred's book, and as much as I knew about baseball cards, Fred knew a lot more than I did, and he wrote our card column for several years.

I had begun to realize that there were folks who knew as much (and possibly more) about baseball than I did, and in May of 1991 I actually, for the first time, let someone else write the cover story for that issue. It was an article on the return of Dwight Evans to Boston as an Oriole, and it was by Mike SanClemente, who did a lot of writing for me in the early years but often used his *nom de plume*, Captain Baseball.

Mike was an indispensable member of our staff in those years, and he didn't mind taking his turn outside the ballpark, yelling and selling. But the price was steep — he was constantly trying to rope me into his Strat-O-Matic league.

We also added statistical splits from STATS, Inc. for selected Red Sox and visiting players — left/right splits, home/road splits, stats by month and by opponent.

To support all this I made an effort to try and sell more advertising. I hired an advertising manager, William Barbera, although 'hired' is a misnomer because he was working on straight commission. He brought in a few new ads, we continued to sell ads to the businesses around the ballpark, and we even sold an ad to Boston's far-flung affiliate in Elmira, NY.

Clyde Smoll was the owner of the Elmira Pioneers, and in a few years, he would make the momentous and highly profitable decision to bring his club to Lowell, where it became the Spinners. But more on Clyde later.

We had a good year in 1991. The Red Sox made a furious late run at the Blue Jays before falling back to tie for second with Detroit, seven games off the pace.

It was the Yankees who stopped Boston's charge. The Sox had come from 11.5 games out to within a half-game of Toronto on September 22, and led New York 5-4 in the ninth inning at Fenway Park. But Jeff Reardon left a fastball over the plate to Roberto Kelly, who hit it out.

In the tenth, Matt Young loaded the bases on eight straight balls and a hit batsman before being replaced by Dan Petry, who surrendered a two-run double to Bernie Williams.

It was a frustrating end to an exciting season. Out on Yawkey Way, we had nearly tripled our sales. Over the course of the season we added even more features, such as complete statistics for Boston's minor league affiliates, which in 1991 were Pawtucket (AAA), New Britain (AA), Lynchburg (A), Winter Haven (A), Elmira (SS-A), and the rookie-level Gulf Coast League club, also playing in Winter Haven. Minor league coverage was rapidly becoming one of our editorial strengths.

During the summer I had also made an effort to expand our prod uct line into amateur baseball. My idea was to publish a program for the Cape Cod Baseball League, a summer league made up of top college players. While the league featured some strong, stable franchises, it also had its share of Mickey Mouse organizations, and I thought that I'd be doing the League a favor by producing a program which could be sold at all league games.

It wasn't a bad idea. However, the execution was poor, I never did get all the clubs on board, and I ended up losing money on the project. It was a learning experience, however, and it kept me busy during the months in the middle of the season when the Red Sox were seemingly going nowhere.

The apathetic play of the Sox had prompted my first negative column — note that it had taken 18 months from the founding of the publication.

*There are still seventy games to play. Anything can happen... That's why we decided to be positive and put Mo [Vaughn] on this issue's cover, instead of something along the lines of "WAKE UP, ELLIS!" or "THINK, LOU!" or "THIS TEAM STINKS, AND THE CONCESSIONS ARE A RIP-OFF!"*

*That last cover idea came to me as I sat in the stands during the final game of the most recent homestand. The Red Sox were losing 10-1 in the fifth inning, their pitcher had already allowed seven walks, the sun was broiling, and Harry M. Stevens was pushing warm, watery Cokes for $1.35 and half-melted "sports bars" for $1.75 a pop. I couldn't for the life of me figure out why there were still 25,000 people in the park.*

There really *were* just 25,000 people in the park. As I write this, the Red Sox have sold out 469 consecutive home dates, but the games weren't all sellouts in the early 1990s. It's been pointed out that there were only 10,454 fans in the stands to see Ted Williams homer in his last at-bat. Well, 25 years later, there were only 13,414 present for Roger Clemens' first 20-strikeout game.

During the early 1990s, the only games that sold out regularly were weekend games. When Clemens was starting, and later Pedro Martinez, there was noticeable jump in attendance, and in magazine sales. Nowadays there are 37,000 people in the ballpark whether it's Josh Beckett or David Pauley, but that's a recent phenomenon.

April was the worst. The ballpark would sell out on Opening Day, which was usually a weekday game, and back then you'd have a week of games that were all 6:05 starts. I've always assumed that because of the cold temperatures that time of year, they wanted to start the games as

September, 1991

early as possible. I'm not sure it made a difference in the temperatures the games were played at, but it sure had an impact on sales.

With a 6:05 start, the few people who can get to the game on time come flying in from work and rush into the park, and everyone else is late and they don't stop for anything — not peanuts, not programs, nothing. That was very discouraging, because normally in April we'd have hired a bunch of new hawkers. They'd start on Opening Day, they'd make some money, and they'd think, "OK, that was fun, this is going to work out pretty well."

And then they'd have three or four games right after that where they'd sell nothing and freeze their pants off and they would just stop showing up.

This is part of my job: blowing sunshine up people's butts, putting a positive spin on everything that's happening around the ballpark. The veteran hawkers would help me out. They'd take the new guys aside and say, "Stick with us, it's getting warmer, it'll get better." But a lot of time the new hires wouldn't have the patience to stick around.

May is no better. It's cold, the kids are still in school, and the schedule is often made up of AL Central and AL West teams which are poor draws.

The end of June, when the kids get out of school, that's when we kick it into high gear. From the last week of June through Labor Day is selling season, and every day is a big day.

After Labor Day, it depends on how the team is doing. If they're in a pennant race, OK. If not, it's tough. The team is playing out the string and so is everybody at the ballpark. It starts to get dark early and the kids and families all disappear and everyone is just waiting to turn out the lights and go home.

Fortunately, we haven't had a lot of that in the last ten years. But during our first few years, when the Red Sox were in a downward spiral, we had some long nights in September.

All this is still true, even though on paper the ballpark is sold out every night. The Red Sox have made an enormous fuss over the sellout streak, but all that means is the tickets were sold. It doesn't mean the fans actually showed up.

Also, just because the announced crowd is steady at 37,000 every night, that doesn't mean sales don't vary, depending on who's in town, who's pitching, what the weather is like, and what time the game is.

Families buy magazines, which is why July and August are our best months and why weekend games are better than weekday games. Saturdays are usually better than Sundays, but only if both are day games. A day game on Saturday sells better than a late afternoon or evening game. Same on Sunday.

And those Sunday 8:05 PM games for television? They might as well play them on a Tuesday night. Nobody brings their kids to a game on a school night that won't get over until 11:30.

On the plus side, the rarity of sellouts back in the early days of the magazine meant that tickets were very easy to come by. People would simply give the tickets to our hawkers as they stood there.

A guy with an extra ticket would walk up and down Yawkey Way trying to sell it, have no luck, and simply hand it to one of my guys. Sometimes they would trade the ticket for a program. If the tickets were any good, the hawker would be in a hurry to count out and get into the ballpark. Occasionally they'd get field box seats, luxury box seats, 600 Club seats. It doesn't happen as often any more, but sometimes the guys do get lucky.

Of course, the tickets are so expensive now, people will go the extra mile to sell them rather than give them away. There are always a lot of tickets and a lot of money changing hands on the streets around Fenway.

Looking over our early issues, the tone is very earnest. We took baseball very seriously. Luckily we had writers like Mark Broitman to keep it light.

Mark, another Penn friend who would soon take over the National League column from Rodney Paul, created a four-page parody of *Baseball Underground* that I would produce here in its entirety if it were not highly inappropriate.

Fred Harris was another guy who helped us keep things in perspective. The baseball card hobby was red hot in those days. There were more card companies introducing more product lines and printing more cards than ever before. Fred was one of the few people writing about the hobby not to get caught up in this.

Fred gave excellent advice, which was to buy older cards, pre-1974, and to be very firm about condition. He also wrote amusingly about such topics as the Topps Company's momentous decision, circa 1992, to stop putting bubble gum in the packs of baseball cards, and about the National Football League.

"Ah, football," Fred wrote. "A savage business."

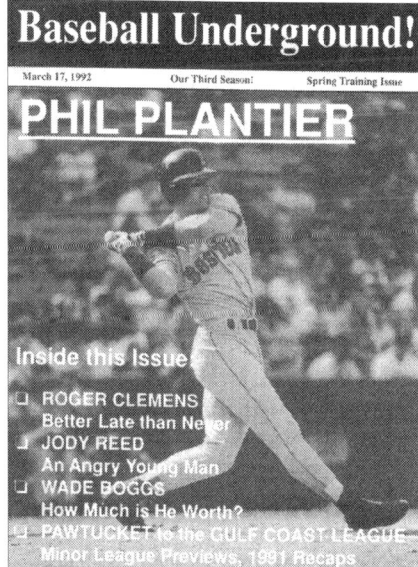

March, 1992: color printing!

During Spring Training, 1992, I discovered that although I continued to be *persona non grata* to the Red Sox, other teams were prepared to accept me as a member of the media, and for the first time I had the experience of covering the game from the inside.

When the Red Sox went on the road, to Lakeland or Sarasota or Bradenton or Dunedin, I was usually able to get a pass. I'd be on the field before the game, taking photos; in the press box grabbing lunch before the game; and hanging around on the fringes of press conferences. I tried to stay out of the way of the Red Sox' PR people. No sense pushing my luck.

Obviously, being on the field for batting practice allowed me to get better photos, especially candids around the batting cage as the players yucked it up with teammates and with players from visiting teams. The spring games usually had a relaxed, informal feel to them, especially for the veterans who knew they'd be heading north with the team. Kirby Puckett and Mo Vaughn were two players who always seemed to be having a good time, hugging friends or signing autographs.

Tim Naehring, then a young infielder battling Luis Rivera for the everyday shortstop job, was a little more intense. One day I noticed he was back after an unexplained absence and I asked him where he'd been.

"I had the flu," Naehring told me. He was sitting on grass in front of the visitor's dugout, stretching.

"The nine-hole flu?" I suggested.

"No," Naehring bristled. "The puking, shitting-out-my-ass flu."

A few days later Naehring was batting with a runner on second. I was in the third-base photo pit, my camera focused on second base, hoping to get a good shot of the runner taking off. Naehring ripped a foul grounder that, focusing on second base, I never saw. Luckily it hit me in the behind and not in the head. When I realized what had happened I picked up the ball and tossed it in my camera bag. It is *verboten*, of course, for media to take souvenirs of any kind, but I still have that ball somewhere, with the black mark on it from Naehring's bat.

One thing that struck me, now that I was on the field with players, was how big they were. I'm 6-0, 180 pounds. You might think from looking at a roster that I'd be about the same size as many of the players. Not so.

There is a big difference between a college professor who is 6-0, 180 and a major-league outfielder who is 6-0, 180. The big leaguer may be the same height, but the composition of his 180 pounds is a lot different. It's muscle on top of swagger.

I had never been around big-time athletes, and I was astounded and intimidated by the size, the strength, and the fitness of the players around the batting cage, not to mention the way they carried themselves and the bat speed they generated. The CRACK of the bat that you hear in the grandstand is a good deal louder heard from the on-deck circle.

Most athletes are pretty good about dealing with the media. I do remember one exception during spring training when I was trying to get a slightly different photo during batting practice, shooting up through the mesh near the front of the cage. Apparently one of the waiting hitters felt I was in the way and started taking practice swings right behind my skull. I felt the whoosh of his bat going by, once, twice. I looked carefully around to find the player glaring down at me, just as another player stepped in and said (to the swinger) "Man, don't do that."

I took the hint and backed off.

But the surly guys you read about from time to time are the exception, not the rule. Of course, there are limits. There are protocols about how and when to approach an athlete for a photo, a question, or a full-blown interview. Twenty years ago, in spring training, things were pretty informal, but nowadays — even more so once the regular season has begun — contact between players and the media is strictly controlled. There is a schedule every day that includes periods when the clubhouse is open and closed, when the manager has reporters in his office, when media can be on the field, and when everyone has to scram.

Passes given to the media are very specific about where that person is allowed to go and what he or she is allowed to do. A pre-game pass allows you on the field during batting practice, but when the cages are wheeled away and infield practice begins, you have to leave the field, and unless you have been comped tickets or have press-box access indicated on your pass, you'll have nowhere to go.

The spring training press boxes, especially 20 years ago, were primitive. Imagine a trailer hanging from the rafters behind home plate. If I had a pass, I would go up after infield and see if there were any press releases or game notes to be had. If there were sandwiches and drinks, great!

If there were a seat open, I might watch the game from the press box, but usually I would go back onto the field and shoot the game. After all, I had only two weeks to get a whole season's worth of photos. If that wasn't allowed I would find the best seat available — preferably between the batter's circle and dugout, with the sun behind me — and shoot the batters and pitchers from there. I didn't get a lot of great shots from that angle, but I got lucky sometimes.

A couple of problems I always had with my spring training photos were the uniforms and the backgrounds. Some big-league teams, including Boston, did not wear their regular uniforms for spring games but rather batting-practice jerseys. No matter how good your photo was, it was obviously a spring training photo, and it looked bush if you ran it in your August issue.

The backgrounds at some parks could be tough. Even if you caught a team wearing their regular uniforms, a line of palm trees in the background could ruin your whole day. We had PhotoShop back then, too, but the computers were much slower and it was painfully time-consuming to edit photos. Still, sometimes there was no way around it.

One terrific ballpark for taking photos was Bradenton, where the Pirates trained in an ancient wooden ballyard right off the street. There was a high, dark-green fence in the outfield that made for a great backdrop that was indistinguishable from a big-league stadium. I loved that park!

Back at Fenway Park that spring, sales were up. The magazine had grown to 48 pages. The writing was better than ever, thanks to the addition of writers like Steve Coe and Tufts righthander Zach Soolman. Zach not only wrote for us, but worked at the ballpark as a hawker, stuffer, and runner. He also helped me out with the production and business end of the magazine. He wore so many different hats for us I listed him in the masthead one issue as "Key Grip."

We started printing and inserting up-to-date stats for the Red Sox and visiting teams into each copy sold at the ballpark, and updated the inserts with each home series. We were on a pace to once again triple our sales from the previous year.

On the field, however, things were getting ugly. The Red Sox still had Roger Clemens to anchor a solid pitching staff, but the offense had evaporated. The Red Sox finished last in their division in batting, on-base percentage, slugging and runs scored.

Realizing the team was going nowhere, GM Lou Gorman dealt Jeff Reardon to the Atlanta Braves at the trading deadline, but the kids he got in return were never big-league regulars. Once again, the Sox' minor league scouting had let them down.

Generally speaking, the success of the Red Sox and of our publication go hand in hand. When the team is winning, attendance is up. People are more interested in reading about a winning team, more likely to want a souvenir, more likely to keep score if the game counts for something.

During the summer of 1992, however, with the team perceived as overpaid and underperforming, I discovered another dynamic, which was that fans gravitated to our magazine and away from the official publication when things were going bad.

One reason was that the official Red Sox magazine was, of course, published by the Red Sox' own public relations department. As a result, it was unfailingly positive and upbeat, regardless of what was happening on the field.

The club was sure to win, the players all loved the manager, respected one another, and got along famously. They were clean-cut, clean-living, God-fearing role models, immersed in rewarding charity work when they weren't working out, eating healthy, or going to bed early. Every minor leaguer was a prospect, every draft pick a future star. The concessions were reasonably-priced and nutritious. The team was devoted to its fans.

There was never anything remotely controversial or challenging. Any talk of salaries or contract status was banned. It was a magazine only a fourth-grader could love.

The official publication was full of stale press releases, photos of the players with their families, snapshots from the Father-Son game, and so on. It was boring at best. But when the team hit the skids, the fan base soon got frustrated with reading the official bullshit. They turned to us. If they were going to spend three hours watching this punchless team lose again, they at least wanted a publication in their hands that told it like it was.

And that's what we did. When the Sox were good, we said so. Bad, we said so.

Our June 1992 issue featured a photo of Roger Clemens and was accompanied by a story which read, in part:

*The fact that Boston has been able to ride Clemens to three divisional titles in the last six years has fooled people into thinking that the Red Sox are a contender. But the truth is that only Clemens makes this otherwise tedious team a potential winner. Without him, they are nothing...*

*The Red Sox may be able to go on like this for a few more years, but the imminent decline and departure of what little supporting cast Clemens has will doom the Red Sox to second-division status as the Rocket enters his thirties. Finally, he will face the last and greatest challenge of being a Red Sox superstar: coming to the ballpark every day and wasting his Hall of Fame talents on a team which, quite frankly, has no chance.*

But we had fun, too. We started a new feature called "Lunch with Lou" that invited people to write to Red Sox GM Lou Gorman — care of us — and published their letters along with a Joe Shea illustration of Big Lou getting ready to chow down on a cheeseburger.

We talked frankly about what the Sox could do to improve themselves. Our constantly evolving coverage of the Red Sox minor-league

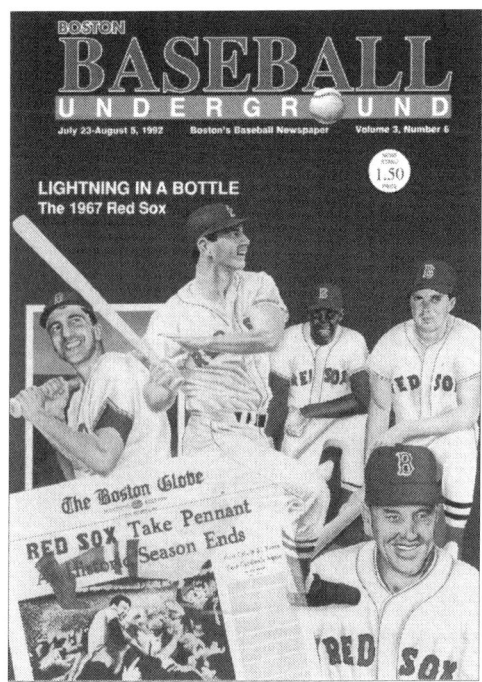

Our first glossy cover: July, 1992. Illustration by Jonathan Banchick

affiliates let people know if help was on the way (it wasn't). And as people began to perceive that there was a competition between us and the Red Sox, a rivalry for their reading dollar, they also understood that they could express their frustration with the team by buying our publication and not theirs.

This competition came to the fore in June of 1992. We had gotten to the point where, as best as I could tell, we were selling just as many magazines as the Red Sox. Finally, the team approached their friends at City Hall to see what could be done.

One day I was stuffing magazines in our decrepit office, the back room of a pizza place on Brookline Avenue named Mom & Pop's. The back room opened up onto an alley that led to Yawkey Way, so it was convenient. The runner came back to me and reported that there was a problem at Gate D — "some guy with a plastic badge and a bad suit" was giving our hawker a hard time, telling him he was going to get arrested, his money and his magazines were going to be confiscated, he was going to have a criminal record...

I ran up to Gate D and found our hawker there, a streetwise black kid named Aaron with a defiant sense of humor. He said someone had shown him a badge and told him that selling the magazine was illegal, that it we couldn't use Roger Clemens' image on the cover, that we were going to get sued by Clemens, by Major League Baseball, all kinds of stuff.

"He asked me my name, so I told him, 'Tyrone'. He says, 'Tyrone what?' So I says, 'Tyrone Shoelaces!'"

I sent the hawkers home, because I didn't want anyone to get arrested, and went looking for the man with the badge. It turned out to be Richard Iannella, Director of the Code Enforcement Police and later a Boston City Councilor.

Code Enforcement is responsible for making sure the City of Boston's various rules and regulations are being followed. Code Enforcement officers, both in and out of police uniforms, were a common sight at the ballpark. It was their job to make sure the food carts were following health codes, trash was being disposed of properly, and so on.

Code Enforcement had never given us any trouble before. Back in 1990, when I launched the business, I had gone to the Boston Police Department and to City Hall to explain what I planned to be doing. I was told that there were no restrictions on selling periodical publications

Kenny French
hawking magazines on
Yawkey Way, July 1992

on public streets, and that my hawkers and I did not require licenses. I had looked up and photocopied the relevant passages from the General Laws of Massachusetts.

At the behest of the Red Sox, however, the City was now telling us to get lost. That was the message I got from Iannella when I found him outside the ballpark. He told me all the same things he had told Aaron, about our being sued by Clemens and by Major League Baseball, adding that *Baseball Underground* was not a publication, but rather a product which required licensing. He advised me that after the end of the home-stand, if we persisted in selling *Baseball Underground*, we would be sub-ject to arrest.

I couldn't believe it! True, the team was bad, but everything else was going so well. The business was taking off. And here were the Red Sox, going behind the scenes at City Hall to put me out of business!

I went home that night thinking that all my hard work over the past two and half years was going right down the drain. But I had one ace up my sleeve.

My mother was a lawyer.

My mother had gone back to school when my sister and I were in high school, attending Suffolk Law School and passing the bar in 1983. She worked in a small private firm downtown. She told me to stick to my guns.

But being right isn't always enough, and you can never have too many lawyers. My father opened his checkbook and arranged for my mother to get some help from Ropes & Gray, a well-known Boston law firm. Together they drafted a memorandum that made my case appear pretty strong.

I was emboldened not only to continue publishing, but to press ahead with my latest improvement, a glossy full-color cover. It was a montage of the "Impossible Dream" Red Sox by local artist Jonathan Banchick, the first of several memorable covers Jon would create for us.

So in July we were back out there, selling magazines, and sure enough the Code Enforcement Police filed a criminal complaint against me on July 1 for occupying city property without a permit, and set a hearing date of July 15.

Already at this stage I was spending more time in the "office" at Mom & Pop's than out on the street selling. Stuffing those inserts into the magazines was taking up a lot of my time. But on July 12 I happened to be selling magazines near the entrance to the 600 Club when a man walked up to me and identified himself as Kevin Cullen, a writer for the Boston *Globe*. He had a copy of *Baseball Underground* under his arm.

"What's this I hear about the City giving you a hard time?" he asked. "I like your magazine. I always buy one on my way into the game. But I just bought this one down the street and the kid who sold it to me says you may have to shut down."

I told him the whole story. When I was finished, he said, "Is that so?"

Two days later, on July 14, 1992, our story was on the front page of the Metro/Region section.

"Sox Look to City to Settle Score" read the headline.

*There is a war going on in the streets that surround Fenway Park. It is a*

**51**

*subtle, soon to be legal, war, pitting one of this town's most venerable and profitable institutions, the Boston Red Sox, against a 27-year-old entrepreneur named Michael Rutstein.*

*Rutstein is the editor and publisher of* Boston Baseball Underground, *a publication hawked outside Fenway that competes with the official Red Sox scorebook sold inside the park.*

*Rutstein's product sells for $1, half the price of the Red Sox publication. Rutstein throws in a pencil for free.*

*For the past three years, the Red Sox were content to mostly ignore the upstarts, although some of the Fenway Park vendors whose commissions have been hurt by the competition have jostled Rutstein's hawkers. In the meantime, Rutstein's publication has gone from 12 pages to 48, from a couple of hawkers to a dozen.*

*And now the Sox have complained to the city, contending Rutstein's hawkers are occupying city property without a permit.*

*Richard Iannella, the city's director of code enforcement, will seek criminal charges in court against Rutstein next week, and rejects characterizing the dispute as a David and Goliath scenario. The Red Sox, he says, are big taxpayers and responsible corporate citizens. Other vendors, he says, like those who peddle sausages and peanuts, pay a fee for space near the park and obey the city's vending plan. Rutstein, says Iannella, pays the city nothing and flouts the city's plan.*

*"People might look at me as a bully," says Iannella, "but this kid says he's selling 1,000 of these things a game. That's $40,000 a season, He's doing OK for himself."*

*This weekend was typical of the cat and mouse game that goes on along Yawkey Way, Boylston Street, Brookline Avenue and Ted Williams Way. Rutstein's hawkers kept moving, stopping only to conduct a sale. Seeing he was losing a potential customer, one hawker played his trump card. "A buck includes the pencil," he said. "Inside, they make you pay a quarter." Sold.*

*Seeing himself as embodying the entrepreneurial sprit that is as American as baseball, Rutstein will invoke the First Amendment to protect his business. And if the Red Sox strategy is to put Rutstein out of business with legal costs, success could prove as elusive as their hunt for a World Series title. Rutstein's lawyer is Susan Rutstein, his mom.*

We had gotten some press coverage already — small articles in the Medford *Transcript*, Middlesex *News*, Brookline *Citizen*, Sudbury *Town Crier*, a nice mention in the Boston *Phoenix*. But with due respect to the tabloid *Herald*, the *Globe* was New England's paper of record, and this story was a big deal for us.

If the Red Sox and Richard Iannella had thought *Baseball Underground* might go quietly, they were about to find out how wrong they were.

The most immediate result of the article was that the City postponed the hearing date, first to July 22, and then again to August 12.

Meanwhile, following the *Globe*'s lead, the story was picked up by the *Herald*, *Baseball Weekly*, *Newsweek*, *BusinessWeek*, WRKO, WEEI, CNN, you name it. A friend of mine on his honeymoon in France opened up an international edition of *Newsweek* and there I was.

"Take These Sox and Shove It — How a publishing rookie routed the home team."

— *Newsweek* headline, August 10, 1992

It wasn't just the amount of coverage, but the sympathetic treatment I received on all sides. The Red Sox had hit the skids, losing seven in a row in late June and falling under .500. Frustration with the team on the field was easily translated into outrage at the heavy-handed way in which the Red Sox had attempted to use their influence at City Hall to put one of their biggest fans out of business.

The media loves a good story, and the Red Sox were not providing many of them that summer. Here was a David vs. Goliath storyline that they could run with, and they did. The City kept putting off the day of reckoning, hoping the furor would die down.

The hearing finally took place on August 12. The media were well-represented, and my answering machine at home was blinking red with

A Harry M. Stevens vendor sets up his program kiosk outside Gate D, 1992

calls from reporters.

My mother and I were met outside the hearing room by Iannella and other city officials, who glanced nervously at the press and ushered us into a private conference room. There, they informed us that the city was dismissing the matter "without prejudice."

That meant the case was closed for the moment, but the City was neither conceding my right to sell the magazine nor waiving its right to return to criminal proceedings at any point in the future.

Robert Cohen, one of the City's lawyers, officially informed us of this in a letter written that very afternoon. The letter further warned me of "Making statements in the course of selling [my] wares which deceive fans… into believing that the product in question is "official" or words to that effect."

This echoed an argument that Red Sox Vice President Larry Cancro had already made. At a loss to explain why thousands of baseball fans would prefer my crude newsletter to their slick glossy magazine, team employees had persuaded themselves that we must be misleading people into thinking that *Baseball Underground* was, in fact, the official program.

We never used the word "official" in any context whatsoever. We weren't trying to fool people into thinking we were the official publication! Our entire business plan was based on our opinion that the official publication stunk, and that ours was better and cheaper. Our sales pitch was built around emphasizing the *differences* between the two publications, not on insinuating that they were one and the same.

I was proud of the product we were selling in 1992, but it was still relatively crude, and unlikely to be confused with any official publication. And if we were tricking people into buying the publication, how did the Red Sox explain our exponential sales growth? Were the fans so stupid that they could be fooled into buying *Baseball Underground* not just once, but over and over? And not just buying it, but subscribing to it? The Red Sox' argument, like their publication, was weak.

I believe the Red Sox knew this all along, and that their accusations were more a matter of saving face than anything else. After all, there must have been some uncomfortable meetings at Fenway Park where the folks responsible for that official program had to explain why sales were down 50%, and how it was that they had lost half their market share to a part-time college lecturer working out of his spare bedroom.

Those folks could have stood up and said, "He's beating us because he works harder than we do" or "He's beating us because he's implemented a bunch of ideas we were too complacent to implement ourselves, even though it would have been easy."

But it was much easier for everyone in the room if instead they stood up and declared "He's beating us because he cheats!"

*Since the city of Boston has informed the Red Sox it does not intend to pursue its licensing case against* Boston Baseball Underground — *the magazine/scorecard sold on the streets outside Fenway Park — the club indicated it will take its own action. While the city is completing its investigation, the Sox announced, the club will sell its publications on the streets as well.*

—Boston *Globe*, August 13, 1992

For the rest of that summer, the streets around Fenway Park were a combat zone. The Red Sox, rebuffed by the City and embarrassed by the media, launched a campaign on two fronts.

Beginning in August, the Red Sox rolled their program kiosks, formerly seen only inside the ballpark, out onto the sidewalks and street corners. There, they competed head to head with *Baseball Underground* hawkers for sales.

This would have been a good plan had the Sox been right about our deceiving fans. After all, with the two publications being hawked side by side, and the Red Sox' hawkers sitting in the high majesty of their kiosks, it was impossible for fans not to understand that these were two competing products, one official and the other, well, underground.

The other idea the Sox came up with was to produce an inexpensive four-page scorecard on card stock and sell it for a quarter. If we could underprice them, well, then they would underprice us!

The media were skeptical.

*This week the Sox began selling the "80th Anniversary Commemorative Scorecard" outside the park for 25 cents. Considering it was unveiled three-quarters through the season and is hooked to an obscure anniversary of Fenway Park, the genesis of the new product is obvious. The Red Sox did not return phone calls. One of their vendors, however, explained the strategy. Asked if he was making money hawking programs for two bits, the vendor replied, "Nah, we're just trying to knock him out," and indicated Rutstein, standing nearby.*

—Boston *Globe,* August 28, 1992

But the 25-cent scorecard never caught on, and the publicity was a godsend. As the Red Sox faded into the pack — they would finish last for the first time in 60 years — our sales remained strong. People who had brushed past us in the past were now intrigued. They stopped and bought the magazine. And a lot of those people were won over.

The publicity also focused attention on our growing readership, and that helped us sell ads. Our new sales manager, Josh Laff, was a talkative, personable kid who took advantage of all that free publicity to triple our ad sales from the year before.

We even began to build up a small list of mail subscribers. It was a market I hadn't really pursued during our first two seasons, first because I had initially conceived of *Baseball Underground* merely as an alternative to the official game program, second because there was already a semi-official Red Sox newsletter being published (*DieHard*) and finally because I hadn't taken the time to figure out the procedures for doing large mailings.

So we started with bulk mail, and what fun my girlfriend and I had sorting the mailings, making up bundles and mail sacks with little color-coded stickers.

But none of these gains would have been possible if not for the efforts of our ballpark sales force. Going head to head with the Red Sox was hard work. It's tough enough to go all out for two hours, holding a heavy stack of magazines, yelling for all you're worth in the hot sun. The Red Sox and Harry M. Stevens came after us very aggressively the last two months of the season, and with all the advantages they had, it was hard not to get discouraged. The Red Sox rolled those big wooden scorecard kiosks out onto the sidewalks, and as Sly would say, it was like tanks against infantry.

Here was the *Baseball Underground* foot soldier, armed with nothing but a t-shirt and an apron, selling a clumsy newsletter for a buck, against the dapper Harry M. Stevens vendors with their slick uniforms, glossy magazine, and imposing kiosks.

We did have a few elements in our favor, however. Thanks to all the publicity, people were looking for us. My hawkers knew that, and they rose to the occasion. They weren't exactly a bunch of wallflowers to start with, of course, but they got louder and prouder as the summer went on, and Harry M. Stevens quickly grew frustrated and dispirited.

I can remember selling magazines outside Gate A and having a Harry M. Stevens vendor come running out of the ballpark behind me and throw me in a headlock. With my arms full of magazines and my apron full of money, I didn't have a chance. As fans began gathering around, however, he had a change of heart. He released me and threatened me with mayhem if I continued to walk up and down in front of "his gate."

Sadly, no members of the media were around. Eventually, he withdrew into the park and I continued hawking in front of Gate A.

Usually it didn't get physical, but each day when the gates opened (we started selling half an hour before that) my hawkers could expect to hear the squeaking wheels of the kiosks as the Harry M. Stevens vendors wheeled them out of the ballpark and into position, right next to my guys. Then they'd try to outyell or outquip one another for two long hours.

I was fortunate to have a very strong group of hawkers that summer, and they were not going to let the Red Sox and Harry M. Stevens beat us. Rather than shirk the challenge offered by the official scorebook, they met it head on.

My father was there for me, as always. One of the qualities that make a great hawker is belief in the product, and my father always had that. It was his belief in me, really. He was a heck of a seller.

Jerry Ferullo was one of our early stars. At first the hawkers had tended to cluster right around the park; one day Jerry asked if he could take a box of magazines and go up to that bridge over the Mass Pike, the bridge over which all the folks came from Kenmore Square. I said he could, and half an hour later he was back, having sold them all. A new "spot" was born.

John Clougherty worked for me for many years and was one of our very best hawkers. A heavyset Irish kid, he did a bang-on impression of Joe Morgan. He held many of our selling records until Sly came along and broke them.

Kenny French and Brian Cloutier were also working for us that summer. Kenny was popular with the other hawkers, but he had a wife who didn't like him hanging around at the ballpark. On the weekends, when they had made a fair amount of money, the older hawkers would usually go out drinking after the game, and sometimes Kenny was persuaded to go along. On day he simply stopped showing up, and nobody could figure out what had happened to him. For years we would make up what-happened-to-Kenny stories.

Chad and his pal Coolidge started working around then. They were great sellers. What everyone remembers about Chad was that one year we had an end-of-season picnic and softball game and Chad, playing the outfield, tried to come in on a line drive and had it tick off his glove and hit him in the eye. Scary, but he was OK.

Jason had come along with John; I hired both kids out of Charlestown High in the spring of 1992. We called him "The Penguin." John, Jason and Lisa, a student at Boston College, were among the very first hawkers who weren't friends or family.

Lisa didn't have the street cred that the rest of our blue-collar hires had, and yet she was a very persistent and effective seller. Her favorite spot was by the entrance to the 600 Club, and because she did so well there, the spot itself got a good reputation, and all the other hawkers wanted to sell there, too. That was "Lisa's Spot" and we continued to call it that long after Lisa had graduated from law school, moved to Chicago, and started working in the District Attorney's office out there.

Edward was a Russian mafia wannabee. One day he brought in a deck of playing cards, and at the end of the day when everyone had gotten their pay, he wanted to cut cards with the other guys for $5.

I said I would cut cards with him, but only if he put down everything he had made that day, about $30. He tried to make it a smaller bet, but I refused, and he couldn't chicken out in front of the other guys. I pulled a queen and took his money, and that was the end of gambling among the hawkers.

Joe was a classic Boston type, a pretty good guy and a very good seller, but not so bright. One day he announced that he had been robbed while he was selling programs, and nobody believed him.

Sly was a rookie that year. He was a sophomore in high school, and hanging out with the older guys — everyone else was in their twenties — was heady stuff for him. Jerry and Chad and Coolidge used to haze him, given that he was a scrawny, hyperactive Italian kid.

One day Sly gave me a nudge in the back while I was off-balance, stacking some boxes, trying to show off in front of the other hawkers. I pushed him back through the office, out the door, down the stairs, into the alley, and fired him.

He'd be back. Sly thrived on the competition with the official vendors, and he would get plenty more opportunities to go head-to-head with them in the future.

While the Red Sox were slow to implement improvements in their publication, they did at least learn one lesson from the PR debacle of 1992.

Approached a year later by a writer doing an article on *Baseball Underground* and other ballpark publications, Jim Samia would only say, "We don't comment on him."

As the 1992 season wound down, the conflict with the City and the Red Sox had a couple of important consequences, First, it established the fact that *Baseball Underground* was not media, as far as the team was concerned, but rather a competing business. That's how they would treat us for the next two decades.

Second, it inaugurated a period of intense competition for market share. While I worked hard to improve the quality of *Baseball Underground*, the Red Sox responded by sending their vendors out into the streets, by introducing a 25-cent scorecard, and by slashing the price of their magazine.

Finally, given the attitude of the team toward my publication and its dismal performance on the field, it meant that the gloves were off as far as criticism of the team and its front office. To that point, I don't believe *Baseball Underground* had been especially negative in its reporting. We didn't go out of our way to bash teams or players; we merely told it as we saw it. There were players we liked and players we didn't like. When things were going good, we said so. When they're weren't, we said so.

Beginning that summer, however, *Baseball Underground* adopted a stance that can only be described as hostile. The Red Sox were portrayed as heavy-handed, greedy, and bumbling.

A good example was a full-page cartoon that appeared toward the end of the 1992 season. The page bore the title "1992 Red Flops" and poked fun at several struggling players — Wade Boggs, Mo Vaughn, Jack Clark, Matt Young — and depicted GM Lou Gorman as Porky Pig, swinging a bucket full of money and declaring, "Th-th-th-that's ball, folks!"

The Gorman-as-Porky Pig motif struck a chord with some fans, and would appear again on a cover the next season. It was funny, in a mean sort of way. Eventually I would grow up enough to regret it.

I do believe the game was passing Gorman by in some respects, but he was a decent man, and it wasn't just him but rather the entire Red

Sox organization that was being passed by. As Tom Seaver had famously said, the Boston Red Sox needed a good flushing.

Still, it was unprofessional to let our off-the-field competition with the Red Sox spill over into our coverage of the team on the field. I just wasn't mature enough, at 28, not to take these it personally when the Red Sox tried to put me out of business!

# 1993

I tried a couple of things that offseason to keep our momentum going. We'd gotten a million dollars worth of free publicity that summer and my plan was to capitalize on it. So when it came time to put out our Winter Meetings issue, which until then had been just eight or twelve pages, we made it a full-size issue. We printed up a bunch of them and planned to hand them out free at the Bruins and Celtics games in December.

It was good issue — Tim Naehring was on the cover — but things didn't go well at the Garden. Even though we were handing them out instead of selling them, the cops and the Garden security wouldn't let us stand inside North Station. We had to stand out on Causeway Street in the dark and the cold, which could really get old after a couple of hours. Fortunately for us, Cepacol had hired some girls to hand out cough drops, so we managed to stay healthy, and I believe Sly got a date with one of the girls.

Handing out things for free is tough, tougher than selling in some ways. When you're handing something out, people assume that since it's free, it must be worthless. They walk right by you. You're not there. If they do register your presence they assume that you're some sort of nut-bag handing out political or religious propaganda; the Scientologists were very active in Boston in those days. Either way, they give you a wide berth.

The hawkers and I were reduced to pleading: "Here, it's a free baseball magazine, take it!" but no, the crowds were too smart for that, and they'd talk right by. It took many nights to hand out all the magazines. Whenever people ask me why we never launched a publication for the Bruins or Celtics, I can tell them exactly why.

Likewise, the Red Sox were opening a new spring training facility in Fort Myers that year, and I had decided to print an expanded Spring Training issue and to hand out copies outside brand-new City of Palms Park. In this I was assisted by Sly, who came down to Florida for a week. Possibly this was the first time he had ever been outside Route 128.

Fort Myers in March was a big improvement over Boston in December. We handed out a lot of magazines and made a lot of friends.

Not surprisingly, the Red Sox turned me down for press credentials, but the cross-town Twins gave me whatever I wanted, and since the two teams often played each other, I was in a better position than ever to cover the team.

I had made a couple of fateful decisions over that winter, between the December Meetings and Spring Training issues. One, I had gotten engaged to Melissa Meyer, my on-again, off-again girlfriend from high school. That's worked out great. My other decision did not work out so well.

As the magazine had gotten bigger and more complex, and as my ambition grew to make the magazine more polished and professional, I realized that it might help to bring in a designer. Up to that point I had been doing everything myself — writing, editing, layout — and although I was competent, I was limited. A designer would give the magazine the professional look I was after, and free me to focus on the writing and editing aspects of the job.

The designer I ended up with was a bright, funny, energetic young guy named Randy English. Randy knew computers, Randy was ambitious, and Randy had personality to spare. He was into music and had a DJ business as a sideline to his design gig, which he ran out of his disheveled apartment in Kenmore Square.

Randy's plan was to "take the magazine digital" by which he meant we were going output film ourselves, with the help of a local service bureau, rather than giving hard copy to the printer to shoot and make film from. In other words, we would assume responsibility for a part of the process that had previously been left to the printer.

The idea was sound, and the service bureau that Randy chose could not have been better. Century Type on Commonwealth Avenue in Boston, not far from my condo in Brookline, was a family business that had been around since the old days of printing and prepress. They began as typesetters in the early 1970s (hence the company name) but had moved with the technology into film and creative services. By the 1993 they were fully immersed in the digital world of print and media, serving as a valuable middleman between clients and printers.

It's hard to overemphasize how much the printing process has changed in our lifetimes. As a high school senior, I was the editor of the school paper. We laid out the paper by printing the stories out in columns, cutting the columns out with scissors, and sticking them with hot wax to a giant piece of graph paper. For making lines and rules, we had skinny strips of black tape.

We had no way to resize or crop photos; we wrote instructions on the back of the photo and let the printer deal with it.

By the time I started *Baseball Underground* in 1990, there were several different programs available so that anyone could do page layout on their personal computer. However, the programs were big, the computers were slow, and it took a long, long time. Still, in theory, you could scan, crop and resize photos, place text, do all sorts of neat tricks with drop caps, rules, shaded areas, and so on, and what you saw on your computer monitor would be what you saw in print.

Usually. Sometimes it would look right on one computer but wrong on another. Other times a file might look fine on the monitor, but wouldn't print right. Or it would print right on an ordinary printer, but at the service bureau, on the film printer, it would look different. There were many variables, most of which I did not understand. Randy understood more than I did and thankfully the folks at Century Type knew a lot more than both of us put together.

The way it worked with Randy was that I would give him stories and photos and he would design the magazine on his computer. He would print the finished pages and then he and I would go back and forth with proofs and corrections. When we had the pages looking the way we wanted, the final files would all go on a disk to Century Type.

Century Type would output the film, and when we had a complete set of film — one sheet of film for a black-only page, four sheets for each four-color page — we would send the film to the printer. Presumably the printer was grateful to be receiving camera-ready film instead of a pile of diskettes.

It was a good system, except that Randy suffered from an organizational dysfunction that made it very difficult for us to remain on schedule without staying up all night two or three days in a row.

Randy had grandiose design ideas, and some of them were very good. However, he would also waste half a day wrestling with a special effect or a 3D rendering while our timetable went out the window. Randy was more interested in pushing the design envelope than with creating a consistent, recognizable design for the magazine. The result was some spectacular layouts but zero consistency from one page to another. When you turned the page of our magazine, you really had no idea what you'd see next.

I remember Randy spending hours on a complex layout, and

Century Type printing sheet after sheet of expensive film trying to get it to output correctly. Finally, Randy had to modify his layout to get it to print. Meanwhile, the bills mounted, time slipped away, and we all lost patience with each other as the print rep hopped up and down, waiting to get his hands on the film.

The chaos and the sleepless nights finally got to me. Luckily, the people at Century Type had seen it all before, and when I was ready, they helped me transition from Randy to a better organized, more professional designer, Marie Haines.

Marie was exactly what the magazine needed. She redesigned the entire magazine to give us a readable, consistent, no-nonsense look. By July of 1993, sleepless nights were a thing of the past, and we had a professional-looking publication that we could be proud of. Many of Marie's ideas are still being used in the magazine today.

Outside the ballpark there was still a certain amount of chaos. The Red Sox hadn't given up, and although their 25-cent scorecard did not return in 1993, the team did take unprecedented steps to try to retake lost ground.

They added some minor league coverage, redesigned their scorecard, and started inserting stats — all features that had been a part of *Baseball Underground* from the beginning. But most significantly — drumroll, please — they dropped the price of the official scorebook magazine from $2 to $1.

It was the first time in memory that the price of anything at Fenway Park had gone down, and a fresh source of terrific, positive publicity for *Baseball Underground*.

If anyone in the Red Sox or Harry M. Stevens organizations had truly thought that the fans bought *Baseball Underground* because they were tricked into thinking it was the official program, that bubble was burst during the last months of the 1992 season. During that time they had sold the official program side by side with *Baseball Underground*, where everyone could see the differences between the two books, and they hadn't been able to cut into our sales at all.

Since the City showed no further interest in challenging our right to sell on the streets around Fenway, and since sending the official scorecard vendors outside to compete with us had not worked, the Red Sox were going to have fight us on features and price, like any other company in a competitive environment.

Competing on features didn't work out for the Red Sox, although it should have. Nobody was in a better position than the Red Sox to put out a superior product; they had the best possible access to players, coaches, and staff. They all the resources they could ask for. But the people who were putting together the official magazine didn't understand what the fans wanted, and never bothered to find out.

Their minor league coverage was two pages. Their redesigned scorecard was still far inferior to ours, because they refused to give up the money from the Budweiser ad that took up so much room. Also, they continued to print it on glossy rather than offset paper, forcing scorekeepers to use pens.

Finally, the stats on their insert were several days old. As I told WEEI's Jimmy Myers on the air that summer, they couldn't be bothered to stay up late the night before the homestand started in order to get the latest stats.

My stat insert, on the other hand, now took up both sides of a legal-sized sheet with stats, numerical rosters, game notes, and player photos.

But the Red Sox' improvements were a token gesture. It was their price cut that they expected to put me out of business and re-establish the monopoly that they had enjoyed for the previous 80 years.

They had decided that there were three possible reasons a fan would buy *Baseball Underground*: because he or she was tricked into thinking it was the official program; because *Baseball Underground* offered a few features that (until now) the official scorecard had not; or because the price was lower.

In their minds, having addressed all three of these issues, they had solved their problem.

But game after game, homestand after homestand, month after month went by, and the problem did not go away: more people were still buying *Baseball Underground* than were buying the official program.

We sold 143,000 magazines in 1993, more than ever before, despite the increased competition and despite the fact that fact that the team finished fifth.

The logical conclusion would be that the fans simply liked *Baseball Underground* better. But the people responsible for the Red Sox' publication could not accept that, and so for years they continued to try variations on the same themes.

There would be years where they would try to add new features, or improve existing features in the magazine. They would get frustrated and send their hawkers back out onto the streets to compete side-by-side with us.

When new ownership took over in 2002, they looked at sales of their magazine and said, "This can't be right." And the cycle started all over again.

In 2003, the City granted the Red Sox exclusive control over Yawkey Way on game days and banished the street vendors, including my hawkers, to less desirable locations.

The Red Sox made a few token improvements to their product, and once again herded the junior vendors out onto the street to compete with our hawkers. Some made an honest effort; others hid in doorways until it was time go back inside and make some real money.

The results were the same. *Baseball Underground* set new sales records while the official program went begging. The Red Sox have never been able to reclaim their lead in the scorecard market.

Contrast this to the experience David Hill and David Simone had in Baltimore.

A year after I launched *Baseball Underground*, they came out with a similar publication called *GameDay*. With the opening of Camden Yards

The author hawking on Yawkey Way, circa 1993

in 1992, their timing was spectacular. What's more, the team embraced them. Not only did *GameDay* receive full press credentials, but they worked out an arrangement with the Orioles to produce and sell their spring training magazine.

Within a few years of launching their publication, David and David were playing hoops with Brady Anderson, while we at *Baseball Underground* continued to work out of the back of a pizza parlor.

*GameDay* — now called *Outside Pitch* — is still being published, and if you're ever at Camden Yards, I recommend picking up a copy.

The stat sheets that we inserted into every magazine sold at the ballpark were a great idea, and all these years later we still use them. The insert is the first thing fans look at when they buy the magazine at the ballpark. Once advertisers caught on to that, we were able to sell advertising on the insert to recover our printing and stuffing costs. Still, when I came up with the idea, I never considered how many hours of my life would be spent stuffing them into the magazines.

Since the insert changed every time a new team came to town, most of the stuffing was done on the day of the game, sometimes under intense pressure. I'd be stuffing as fast as I could for two, three hours at a stretch as the runners came and went, snatching away the boxes of mag-

April, 1993. Note the barcode in the lower left corner. We were taking our first stab at newsstand distribution

azines as fast as I could fill them. I could stuff ten or twelve boxes an hour, which is 1200-1400 magazines, but on a good day, they were selling faster than that. We might sell 1500 magazines in a hour.

Stuffing soon became paid work. I paid a dollar a box, and the guys who were good at it could come in early and make $20 or more before we even started selling. That was decent money in 1993 when the minimum wage was something like $4 an hour.

Unfortunately, we were stuffing in the back room of Mom & Pop's — a nasty place on a hot summer day. There was no air conditioning. There were buckets of grease congealing in the back room with us, racks of stale bread destined to be turned into croutons, and leaking bags of food garbage going rancid in the heat.

The other disadvantage to Mom & Pop's was that although the storefront was at street level, the back room was up a flight of stairs from the alley below. When the truck delivered the magazines, we had to set up a bucket brigade down the alley and up the stairs, passing the heavy boxes from hand to hand until they were stacked up to the ceiling. Hard work.

During the 1993 season, I had a chat with J. P. Plunkett, the sports editor of Boston College's student newspaper, *The Heights*. J.P. had been doing some college baseball coverage for us, and he believed that there was an opportunity over in Chestnut Hill.

For the previous several years there had been an independent newsletter devoted to BC sports called *Eagle Eye*, but it was going out of business. J.P. felt there was a real market for a well-executed publication, and that with the hiring of Tom Coughlin, BC football was headed in the right direction after some down years.

I set up an appointment with the folks in the BC Athletic Department. They assured me that they had a real interest in having an independent publication devoted to BC sports — with the emphasis on independent.

Because recruiting plays such an important role in college athletics, and because colleges and coaches are barred by the NCAA from discussing recruiting, there's an opportunity for independent publications to serve both the fans and the school. BC was more than willing to give us credentials and to do whatever they could, within the rules, to get our new publication off the ground. The recruiting information we'd have to get ourselves.

*Eagle Action* launched in September as a subscription-driven magazine very similar in appearance to *Baseball Underground*. The magazine format would turn out to be too expensive for the size of the market, and after a few years *Eagle Action* became a newspaper. We also set up an 900 number where callers could get up-to-date information on BC sports and recruiting.

Eventually the 900 market was replaced by the internet, and after ten years of publication, the newspaper itself was replaced by a premium website on the Rivals.com network, recently acquired by Yahoo.

Fifteen years later, EagleAction.com is going strong, offering more and better BC sports and recruiting information than has ever been available before. The real challenge, apart from the change in formats, has always been getting the best and latest recruiting dope. For that I have been indebted to a series of excellent recruiting analysts, from Tom Grace to Kevin McGrath to Mike Farrell.

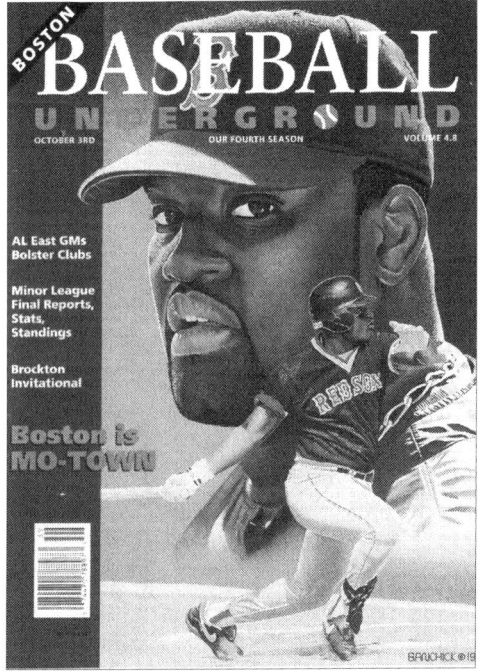

October, 1993. One of our best early covers. Illustration by Jonathan Banchick

# 1994

For two years *Baseball Underground* had been urging the Red Sox to sack General Manager Lou Gorman, and in 1994, the team finally did so.

*Baseball Underground* hailed Gorman's replacement, Dan Duquette, as a savior. Our April issue contained a full-page illustration depicting Duquette as Indiana Jones, with the legend "Raiders of the Lost Park."

On page two we ran a box with a head shot of Duquette labeled "Our Hero". The box was subdivided into three sections:

The Man
The Moves
The Miracle of the Month

Duquette was a Massachusetts native. He had cut his teeth with the small-market Milwaukee Brewers and Montreal Expos, where he had earned the reputation of being a guy who could do a lot with a little. He was a young guy who looked as if he knew how to turn on a computer, and he vowed to overhaul the Red Sox' parched farm system, a project close to my heart.

We gave Duquette our unreserved support for his first few years as GM, including a free pass for 1994. We understood it would take several years to get the organization turned around, and in the meantime we applauded Duquette's purging of the scouting and coaching ranks.

It was a given that the Red Sox would stink that season. Only two factors conspired to keep the team from finishing seventh. First, the American League had been reorganized into three divisions, which meant that fifth place was as low as you could sink. Second, the season ended on August 12 with a strike, just as the team was going belly up. They finished fourth at 45-61, just a game ahead of the Tigers and already 17 games behind New York.

Boston's pitching remained respectable, but the offense was weak. In retrospect, in the Year of No World Series, being any better would have been a waste of effort.

Our sales were flat, reflecting the team's poor performance and the threat of the strike, and ad sales were down, but there were a couple of

bright spots in the gloom.

Marie Haines had finished her complete redesign of the publication, bringing a clean, consistent look to the magazine now known as *Boston Baseball*.

I changed the name because I was no longer content to be a subversive newsletter, nipping at the heels of Red Sox officialdom. I had greater ambitions for the magazine. Our sales were such that we were reaching a wide audience, an audience we could market to advertisers and use ourselves to sell merchandise, travel packages, and fan club memberships. In short, we could take advantage of all the opportunities that the Yawkey Trust ownership was content to ignore. It was time to shed the *Underground* moniker and move into the sports marketing mainstream.

The name change was symbolic of my ambition to do all these things, but as it turned out, changing the name was a lot easier than getting our new marketing plan off the ground.

It's tough to sell anything when the team is losing. Having tried and failed to build a partnership with Twins Enterprises, the nationwide souvenir giant that controls the souvenir shops and carts around Fenway Park, I decided that I would try to sell Red Sox merchandise through the magazine. I set up an account with Majestic, an MLB-licensed apparel manufacturer, and drafted my wife to serve as the model. We sold Red Sox uniform jerseys, warmup jackets, and sweatshirts at very reasonable prices, but sales were slow.

Inside the magazine, we continued to put more resources into our minor league coverage, expecting that Dan Duquette would rebuild the farm system and that interest in the team's prospects would rise. I began writing a new minor-league overview called Around the Minors, a task that I really enjoyed.

Around this time Fred Harris began to scale back his contributions, and Tom DiGiandomenico took over some of the baseball-card coverage. In time, Tom would become our longest-running contributor, wresting that honor from Ron Marshall in 2008.

And although it was not a spectacular year for ad sales, we did strike a deal with Red Sox batting coach Mike "The Hit Man" Easler to promote his new instructional video. Easler's ad ran on our back cover for most of the season, and his people invited me to Fenway to do an interview with him.

It was my first time inside the park as a member of the media. It must have been early in the afternoon, because I remember the ballpark being empty. I entered through the player's parking lot and found Easler under the stands. As we headed for the field, we bumped into my new hero, Duquette. He gave me a clammy handshake and moved on. I should have known then that it wasn't going to work out.

Out on the field, I snapped some photos as Easler worked in the center-field batting cages, and someone snapped a few photos of me in left field, where my man Yaz used to roam. That was a good day.

But after the season ended abruptly in August, I waited a few weeks, then began hauling my unsold magazines, one carload at a time, to the dumpster behind my condo. Baseball was in limbo, the owners and players were far, far apart, and the fans grew increasingly alienated as the strike dragged on, canceling the remainder of the season and finally the postseason as well.

Thank goodness for *Eagle Action*, and for Emma Dorton Rutstein, born on March 11, 1995, seven pounds and 20 inches.

July, 1994

# 1995

Nothing was cleared up over the winter and early spring. President Clinton's demands for a settlement went unmet. The strike continued, and the owners opened their training camps with replacement players.

Having already made my travel arrangements, I went to Florida in March and shot roll after roll of players I had never heard of and, for the most part, would never see again.

By the time a settlement was reached, it was too late to play a full 162-game season. A revised 144-game slate was put in place, and the players returned to rush through an abbreviated spring training. The Red Sox played their home opener on April 26, to scattered boos.

Fans were bitter about the prolonged strike, and 1995 could have been a struggle for us. However, this was when Dan Duquette proved his worth. Duquette took advantage of the chaos that followed the resolution of the strike to snap up useful players. Best of all, he signed a struggling knuckleballer from the Pirates organization named Tim Wakefield.

The Red Sox bounced back from their awful 1994 season to go 86-58, the equivalent of winning 97 games over a full season. The pitching continued to be a strength behind Roger Clemens, Erik Hansen, and Wakefield (16-8, 2.91 in 27 starts), but it was the turnaround of Boston's offense that made all the difference. Mo Vaughn produced an MVP season, supported by John Valentin (102 RBI) and Jose Canseco (.306-24-81).

As a result, *Boston Baseball* broke all previous sales records in spite of the shortened schedule and the fact the Red Sox were still selling their official magazine for $1.

We also sold more ads than ever before, with Bradlees taking over the back cover, the first time we had been able to attract a major regional chain. That was a big step for us, and (in my mind) an endorsement of our mainstream strategy.

One positive result of the strike was that the Red Sox, fearing the backlash from the fans and media, proved much easier to deal with. In June, they granted me a pre-game field pass for a game against the Mariners, the first time I had entered Fenway Park with a press pass.

Never having worked a big-league game before, I assumed that it would work something like spring training. That being the case, I made sure I was the first photographer on the field, and I walked over to the first-base photo pit and put my camera bag on the preferred position, closest to the Red Sox dugout. Then I went and shot roll after roll of the Sox and Mariners stretching and taking batting practice. I made certain to get some good shots of young Seattle stars Ken Griffey Jr. and Alex Rodriguez.

When the grounds crew wheeled away the batting cage, I headed back for the photo pit, planning to shoot fielding practice. But my camera bag was not where I had left it.

Apparently, first-come, first-served was the rule in spring training, but in the big leagues, seniority rules. The *Globe*, *Herald*, and AP photographers had moved my bag out onto the infield dirt and taken the three available positions.

I chalked it up to a lesson learned, collected my bag, and walked up into the stands. Had I known that I wouldn't get another press pass for twelve years, I might have made more of a fuss.

Incidentally, the Red Sox did not raise ticket prices for 1995. The next time that would happen would be 2009, when the meltdown of the housing and credit markets forced the team's hand.

May, 1995

The 1995 season saw Tufts students Zach Soolman and John Tomase writing more stories for us. It marked the *Boston Baseball* debut of Glenn Stout, who was to become our most popular and controversial columnist.

That season also saw the debuts of Aaron Sele and Jeff Suppan, who would go on to enjoy long major-league careers. For both hurlers' big-league debuts, we printed up a special insert, a practice that the fans loved and which has always been great for sales.

At midseason, we moved out of Mom & Pop's Pizza and across Brookline Avenue into a defunct auto-parts store and warehouse. We had gotten along well with the people at Mom & Pop's, but one day a TV station dropped by to do a story on me. When the pizza guys saw the cameraman filming in their back room — a smorgasbord of health-code violations — they freaked.

Luckily, we landed on our feet across the street in an empty auto parts warehouse. The space worked out great for us, and the next year, when VIP Parking bought the building and cleaned it out to park cars, we were able to stay on in the back. Sadly, Paul Mattes of VIP would no longer allow the hawkers and I to play wiffleball in the building, on account of the fluorescent lights we were likely to break.

We would be based out of this building for the next 14 years. The building itself had not been used for some time; it was full of dirt, debris, and junk. The basement was flooded and full of rats. But it was close to the ballpark, and it was at ground level, which made deliveries easier.

We took a corner of the building, stacked the boxes of magazines almost to the ceiling, and assembled an office out of castaway furniture and broken swivel chairs. The garage was in constant use, and there was no way to lock up our gear, so we couldn't leave anything that might be stolen. We listened to the games on a crappy old transistor radio, in the hope that we could leave it out without it being taken. Eventually it did get stolen, but only after several years, at which point we adopted another crappy radio.

On the other hand, our solar-powered calculator, which hasn't seen the sun in a decade, has never been stolen and continues to work admirably. That calculator and Rodney Paul's clipboard have combined to give me 35 years of service.

Speaking of long years of service, it was around this time that John Ovesen, also known as Lemon, and Hai Ho Nguyen came to work for me.

They were spending a lot of time around the ballpark already, coming down early and hanging around the player's entrance for autographs. It was big business back then — still is — and as Hunter Thompson once said, when the going gets weird, the weird turn pro. At the age of twelve or thirteen, Hai and Lemon were already flipping autographed items for money. They worked Fenway Park, the Boston Garden, the team hotels, and the clubs, restaurants and malls where visiting players were likely to be found. They went after musicians as well as athletes, staking out concert halls and clubs. They were paparazzi, but with Sharpie pens instead of cameras.

Since their autograph-hunting took them all over the map at odd hours, it's easy to conclude that these two boys were undersupervised. They were. They were also two of the best, hardest-working kids you can imagine, and mature beyond their years. When they came to me and asked for work I knew that they'd be able to handle anything I asked them to do. Initially, that was stuffing inserts and running, although later they both became excellent hawkers also. They could be trusted to be there for a truck delivery, to unload and stack the magazines, pick up the inserts from the printer, even run the entire operation for me if I needed to be somewhere else.

Lemon grew up in Roslindale and knew all along he was going to have to work for anything he got. He is one of the hardest-working people I have ever known. He would do whatever I asked him to do — stuffing, running hawking, unloading trucks — and volunteer to do more. He was never sick, never gave an excuse, never complained about anything.

He would show up early and sweep the office. He would pick up work on one of Twins Souvenir carts, with one of the sausage vendors, or for my landlords at VIP Parking. Show Lemon the money, and he would bust his ass for you.

Lemon has a story he likes to tell about his first day working for me. He says he introduced himself to me and stuck out his hand, but that I turned away without shaking it. If that really happened, it certainly wasn't intentional, but he's still giving me crap about it 14 years later.

The part he doesn't tell is that he lied to me about his age. Lemon was very tall kid for his age, and he told me he was in high school when he was, in fact, twelve.

Hai was a year or two older. He and his family were "boat people"

Lemon hawks BB
on the beach in Thailand

who had left Vietnam for the Philippines and eventually the United States.

Hai had a rare illness that affected his digestive tract and for which he was operated on over and over again. Being in and out of hospitals, and being told that he shouldn't plan on a long life, Hai had a unique perspective. He liked to have fun, he could laugh at anything, including himself. He was a very smart kid, something of a philosopher, intellectually curious, and even-tempered.

The hawkers like to make fun of his accent and his curious grammar, which includes random pluralizations. Sometimes he says things that make no sense. Maybe it's all the anesthesia that has been pumped through him.

One day I had an advertiser visit me in the garage. The hawkers were getting ready to go out and sell when the advertiser walked in, wearing a blazer and an ascot.

The hawkers fell silent. I don't think they had ever seen an ascot outside of the movies. Normally, the hawkers are a lively bunch as they're getting ready to work. There's a lot of laughing and joking around. But there was dead silence while this guy and I carried on our conversation.

Finally we finished talking and said our good-byes, all in the middle of this silence that had become palpable. The hawkers were just staring at us. And as the guy turned to go, Hai blurted out, "Yeah, don't eat too much caviar!"

Eventually the other hawkers all came to appreciate Hai's intelligence and impartiality — he never was one to bear a grudge — and he ended up with a role that was somewhere between Court Jester and Voice of Reason.

He and Lemon had found each other early on, outside the players' entrance, and they were inseparable during all their years of autograph-hunting. Once Lemon was out of high school, they agreed that they wanted to see the world. Six months out of the year they stalked celebrities and sold magazines; the other six, they traveled to Europe, Asia, and South America.

Their budget was limited, but still they went everywhere and did everything, sleeping in hostels and train stations and hooking up with other penniless wanderers wherever they went. They got pretty smart about finding deals, about traveling on the offseason. Lemon went to Iceland in December one year. He claims he had a great time.

I was jealous as hell, but they did bring me coins from each country they visited. They also amused themselves by taking photos of themselves holding up copies of *Boston Baseball* in exotic locales — on a bridge overlooking Hong Kong, on a beach in Indonesia, at a

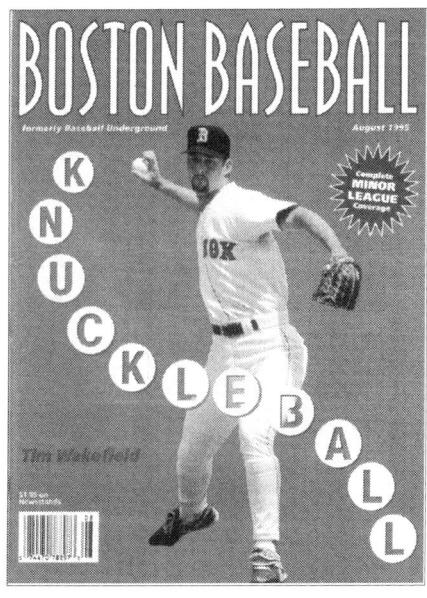

May, 1995.
The hawkers loved this cover

Cambodian temple.

They came back from Southeast Asia with straw rice-paddy hats — two for my kids, and two for themselves. They'd wear the hats while they were pushing the dollies around the ballpark. I can remember Hai hawking on a street corner, wearing his hat and shrieking "Free bag of rice with every program!"

One year they had a falling out while they were traveling and they came back not speaking to each other, but mostly they got along.

Finally Lemon came back from one trip with a Taiwanese girlfriend, which upped the ante, and then Nikki came to visit him in the US, where she was employed by Hai in the book-selling business he built from scratch. The boys were growing up. Lemon spent a year in Taiwan teaching English to be with his girl, and Hai worked to build his own business, but still they came to the ballpark — Lemon for the camaraderie and for the cash, Hai mostly for the camaraderie.

My fondest memories of *Boston Baseball* are not the days we sold the most magazines but the afternoons spent stuffing magazines with Lemon and Hai, before anyone else was around, with the garage doors open to let the air in, talking about everything under the sun.

One of our star hawkers at this time was Jeff Brink. Jeff was an older guy with a real twinkle in his eye, a chef at MIT. He had tried to start his own restaurant as a younger man and lost a large amount of money.

We called Jeff "The Evil Wizard" because he had a wicked sense of humor and liked to take a drink now and then. He was not intimidated by Sly and would give as good as he got.

One night, when Jeff may have had a few drinks, he counted out early and went up to the Bridge where Sly was still selling to the late-comers. They had been arguing about something beforehand, and now Jeff came up behind him, grabbed Sly's hat, and threw it off the bridge onto the Mass Pike below. Sly started punching him and I believe someone had to call a cop to come break it up.

I liked Jeff, but he was a pessimist. At the beginning of every month, when the magazines would get delivered and be stacked up to the ceiling, Jeff would come in and say "Holy crap! How are we going to sell all of these?"

Two weeks later, after we'd sold off a lot of the stock, he'd come in, look around, and say, "Mike! Are we going to have enough magazines?"

Zach's younger brother Jonah was also working for us. He was too quiet for a hawker, but he was a tennis player with strong legs, so he was well suited to being a runner. He used to literally run with the magazines, which could lead to problems on busy days when he might have 100 pounds of magazines stacked on his dolly.

One time he nearly ran down Roger Clemens as the Rocket was returning from a jog around the Fens. Many of the pitchers used to jog around the neighborhood in those days, unnoticed by the fans. You'd have Clemens or Derek Lowe jogging down the street in a sweaty t-shirt, and nobody would bat an eye.

As always, the *Boston Baseball* writers continued to make an independent contribution to coverage of the Red Sox. In June, we called for a change in the All-Star Game format to a Ryder Cup-style event, pitting North American players against those from the rest of the world.

In August we began an ongoing campaign to extend the format of baseball's postseason series, arguing that baseball's best teams haven't played a six-month season just to roll the dice in a short five- or seven-game series.

By the end of the year, thanks to Boston's surprising division title, the Red Sox were back in the good graces of its fans. Not even the team's quick elimination at the hands of the Cleveland Indians could diminish anticipation for 1996. With our new GM and revamped line-up, it seemed anything was possible.

# 1996

Yes, anything was possible — including one of the worst starts in franchise history. The Red Sox lost 12 of their first 14 games and didn't get back to .500 until late August. They wound up at 85-77, in third place, seven games behind the Yankees.

Sales were down only slightly, as we fielded a strong new crop of hawkers. Jerry, Chad, Coolidge and Kenny were gone. Sly was going strong — he was the top seller for all five issues in 1995 and five of our six issues in 1996. Tim Michaud was still selling, with his friend Chris and his girlfriend, Heidi.

Chris was a piece of work. I never saw anyone who could yell that loud with a cigarette between his lips. I was always after him not to smoke while he was working. Chris was famous for having his cash be short the exact price of a sausage and soda.

Chris also worked for *Eagle Action*, as did several of my regular baseball hawkers. We used to sell the newspaper on BC football game days at the satellite parking lots where people could park and take shuttle buses to Alumni Stadium.

On one of these days it rained, and Chris left his newspapers uncovered. He brought them back to me as a soggy papier-mache mess. I was so mad that I deducted the cost of the ruined newspapers from his pay for the copies he had managed to sell. His net worked out to ten cents, so I fished a dime out of the ashtray of my car and gave it him. The other hawkers just fell down laughing, and the incident passed into *Boston Baseball* lore.

*Boston Baseball* had now grown to 56 pages. Tony Massarotti was writing our cover stories, a valuable connection for us because he had credentials through the *Herald*.

We had also added two new columnists in Mark Scapicchio and Doug Pappas, the chairman of SABR's Business of Baseball committee.

As you might expect, Doug focused on business stories, but he had the gift of explaining things so the stories were never dry. In those times of labor strife, cable expansion, and new ballpark rumors, Doug's were among the most-read stories in the magazine.

Ron Marshall inaugurated a series of where-are-they-now inter-views with former Red Sox players, and Bill Chapman contributed a photo feature each month.

I had met Bill when he invited me to be a guest on his local cable access show; Bill was wearing a Yellow Submarine tie and we immediately hit it off. Bill wasn't a natural-born talk-show host, but he is a true baseball aficionado and an excellent photographer, and soon we were carpooling down to Pawtucket to cover the minor leaguers.

Bill loved shooting baseball and cared little about the money, which endeared him to the folks down in Pawtucket and everywhere else he went. He introduced me to Glenn Stout, Luke Salisbury, Dick Johnson and others, including the wonderfully-named Dick Beverage. I'm pretty sure I first met Glenn at an exhibition of Bill's photographs in a Kenmore Square gallery. Bill has been sober for many years now, but he had arranged for beer and I remember chatting with Glenn over a Pabst Blue Ribbon.

I recall driving down to Pawtucket with Bill one time — he doesn't drive, so he always had to put up with my driving — and telling him, "You know, Bill, there must be something to these 12-step programs. You haven't mentioned the Beatles in an hour!"

Bill Chapman at his summer home — McCoy Stadium in Pawtucket

1996 was the inaugural season for the Lowell Spinners. Over the winter, Clyde Smoll had moved his New York-Penn League franchise from Elmira, NY to Lowell, MA, where the Pioneers became the Spinners.

The Class-A New York-Penn League is a short-season league. The rosters aren't set until mid-June, a week or two after the amateur draft, and the teams play a 76-game schedule that ends around Labor Day. Generally the league is designed to provide a training ground for college players who've just entered the pro ranks. There's also a liberal sprinkling of high school and international players who have worked their way up from the rookie-level Gulf Coast League.

Clyde had owned the Elmira Pioneers since 1983, and for most of that time, his club was a Red Sox affiliate. John Valentin, Tim Naehring, and Mike Greenwell all made their pro debuts with Elmira. Later the Red Sox moved their affiliation to Utica, NY where they played as the Blue Sox from 1993-1995.

I remember driving out to that ballpark in 1993 or 1994. It was pretty rustic: a chain-link backstop, blue-painted plywood dugouts and fences. There was an eight-foot folding table set up at the entrance for tickets sales, and a couple of vending carts for concessions.

Ah, the minor leagues, the way it used to be!

At that time, baseball fans were just catching on to the importance of player development, and there was a surge in interest in the minor leagues. Franchise values soared, minor league hats and shirts became hot items, and *Baseball America*, that valuable publication, could at last be found on mainstream newsstands.

Providing better coverage of the Red Sox' farm system had been one of our founding principles, and I spent a lot of time in the early years tracking down competent people to provide regular coverage of Boston's minor-league affiliates. It wasn't always easy.

At the higher levels, the local daily newspapers covered the teams, and that was where I'd look first. At the lower levels, however, and especially in smaller towns, the team might not have anyone covering them on a regular basis. In that case, I often ended up with the team's PR interns, or even local college students, writing our stories. These kids were usually enthusiastic, and some of them showed promise, but often they were bad, and unreliable to boot.

In those days before everyone had cell phones, voice mail, and e-mail, it could be terribly frustrating trying to track down a writer in

August, 1996

Lynchburg, VA or Battle Creek, MI or Utica, NY with the deadline looming.

But back to Clyde. He was a hard-working guy. Owning a team at that level, in those days, was a hands-on job. I remember watching him tamping down the mound at Alumni Field when he was well into his fifties.

Well, Clyde worked out a deal to move his team to Massachusetts, where it would become a Red Sox affiliate once again. This was part of a concerted effort by the Red Sox to bring their affiliates home to New England. This was not only more convenient but made great marketing sense. Boston's affiliation with the Double-A Portland (ME) club a few years later meant that three Boston farm teams were now playing within a two-hour drive of Fenway Park.

Lowell was Red Sox Country, all right, but the transition would not be an easy one. Clyde's club would initially play at Alumni Field off Route 38, which wasn't a whole lot better than the park in Utica — a chain-link backstop with a plywood fence and aluminum bleachers. At least there were trailers for the clubhouses, concessions, and team offices. And there were plans in the works to move the Spinners to a new ball-park on the Merrimack River, which they would share with UMass-

Lowell.

The Spinners came to town during the 1995-96 offseason and opened an office in downtown Lowell. They were behind the eight ball in terms of selling tickets and sponsorships, and they welcomed my offer to produce a program for them. Our written agreement, which fit on one page, stated that I would produce and sell a 92-page program at no cost to the Spinners; they were allotted 60 pages to sell advertising and they got to keep that revenue. It was very similar to the offer I would soon make to the Red Sox.

We worked together for three years. During the first two years, when the team was playing at Alumni Field, we didn't make much money. The program sold for $2 and we only sold a couple of hundred per game.

Still, it was fun working on the inside for a change. The Spinners were good to us. Our reporters and photographers were welcomed. Maura Porter was our first Lowell beat writer, and Bill Chapman spent a lot of time in Lowell during the Spinners' first few seasons.

With the signing of an agreement to put the Spinners into a brand-new HOK-designed facility by 1998, Clyde decided the time was right and sold the team to Drew Weber. The Spinners played one more season at Alumni Field, and then moved to LeLacheur Park. Attendance immediately doubled, and the Spinners have been filling that ballpark ever since.

With the new park, it was now possible to make money on the programs, but with the move to the downtown location, it was harder than ever to get my hawkers from Boston to Lowell. Often we didn't have enough hawkers to take advantage of the sold-out crowds, and communication between ourselves and the team wasn't as good as it had been in previous seasons.

After the 1998 season, the

Johan selling programs at the Spinners' first home, Alumni Field

Spinners decided to produce their own scorecard, but we have continued to swap ad space for tickets and promotional considerations. My nine-year-old son Jake threw out the first pitch at a 2006 game as a representative of *Boston Baseball*. It was a fun day for both of us.

The Red Sox' slow-but-steady recovery from their disastrous start in 1996 had fans optimistic for 1997. But the team lost 13 of 15 in May and never got back to .500. Though the offense was decent, the pitching sagged without Roger Clemens, who had never gotten along with Duquette and was allowed to leave via free agency after the 1996 season.

With the departure of Clemens and of Mike Greenwell, no players remained who had been in the roster when *Baseball Underground* was launched in April of 1990.

We did have some fun in 1997 despite the struggles of the team. I'd sent Glenn Stout to Red Sox Fantasy Camp over the winter, and he wrote entertainingly about his camp experience. Coke bottles had sprouted up over the Green Monster, and everyone had an opinion. Wally the Green Monster made his debut at Kids Opening Day and was roundly booed, prompting the Red Sox to scale back their plans for the new mascot.

Ron Marshall hooked up with former Red Sox infielder Jerry Remy for a Q&A series that would be a staple of our coverage for years to come. Jerry was independent and opinionated enough to fit in with *Boston Baseball*, and those qualities would soon make him the star of the team's cable broadcasts.

We also experimented that year with a series of articles by Mike Gimbel, Dan Duquette's infamous "StatMan". Gimbel had received his fair share of abuse in the mainstream media, and he was an odd character. However, he was also a very bright guy who had given deep thought to the statistical analysis of baseball, and his articles gave us some insight into Duquette's decision-making process.

Duquette was definitely a guy who studied the Bill James and STATS, Inc. publications that were becoming popular. I remember flying out to watch the Arizona Fall League games when Nomar Garciaparra was playing for Scottsdale. As I boarded the flight to Phoenix, I noticed Duquette sitting in the cabin, but I decided not to pester him. As it turned out, I had two open seats next to me, and after takeoff Duquette moved over to take the aisle seat in my row.

I was reading the STATS Inc. *Minor League Handbook* in paperback.

Duquette smiled and reached into his briefcase for the same book — with a spiral binding.

"Ah," I said. "The General Manager's edition."

In July Roger Clemens made his first start at Fenway against the Red Sox, and we handed out free "WANTED" posters with his photo.

**WANTED for TREASON**
**William Roger Clemens**
**alias "The Rocket" alias "Fat Bill"**
**Wanted by Red Sox Nation for various and sundry crimes**
**including treason, speaking with a forked tongue,**
**and generally being a chowderhead**

In truth, you couldn't blame Clemens for leaving, but a lot of fans had taken it hard, and the poster was very popular. We printed up similar posters when Johnny Damon returned as a Yankee. We also inserted special scorecards for the annual visit of the Colorado Silver Bullets, a professional women's baseball team, as well as for the Upper Deck Heroes of Baseball and pretty much any other special event at Fenway Park.

April, 1997

Interleague baseball had debuted at Fenway that summer as the Phillies visited Boston on June 16. Later in the season, we would reap a windfall when the Braves came to town for the first time since the old Boston Braves had left for Milwaukee in 1952.

For the first time, we ran a split cover — two different covers for the same issue, with a Warren Spahn cover for the Braves games, which happened to fall on Labor Day weekend, and a Nomar "Rookie of the Year" cover for the rest of the month.

The Saturday game of that series against the Braves was the best we ever had. We fell just short of 5,000 magazines, and would have sold more had not our system broken down under the strain. Lemon was running magazines out to all the hawkers, racing back to the office to help me stuff more magazines, then rushing them back out, all day long.

Overall, it was another disappointing year on the field, but a good one at the bank. Sales at the ballpark were up, and ad sales hit a new high. I continued to try to extend the *Boston Baseball* brand, but without much success.

Noting that the team's only fan club was the rather exclusive BoSox Club, I proposed a new "Fenway Fan Club" open to all, which offered a subscription to *Boston Baseball*, 20% discounts off merchandise from *Boston Baseball*, Sportsworld, and the Sports Museum of New England, Fan Club outings to Fenway Park, McCoy Stadium and LeLacheur Park, and new member drawings for autographed items and Red Sox tickets. The annual dues were $29.95.

As a package it compares very well to what thousands of Red Sox fans got recently when they joined "Red Sox Nation" but of course I didn't have the marketing muscle of the team behind me. Perhaps fan clubs are one of those things that just taste better with the "official" stamp on them.

In December, times being good, we opted to upgrade the paper stock we using, giving the magazine a whiter, brighter look with a little more heft. We had good news to write about as well — Dan Duquette had dealt Carl Pavano and Tony Armas Jr. to the Montreal Expos for young ace Pedro Martinez, and signed Martinez to a long-term deal.

Now the Red Sox had an ace to replace Clemens. This was the first in a series of moves that would lead to the long-awaited championship in 2004.

Speaking of aces, my son Jake was born on October 21. Last summer he posted a 0.65 ERA for his Little League team. If they had a Cy Young Award in that league, he would have been the unanimous choice.

December, 1997

# 1998

Sometime around 1995 I had met with the Red Sox to discuss the possibility of our working together. The talks didn't get very far.

The team seemed to be offering me a job working on their publications, but the offer was never made clear. If they wanted me to give up my business and come to work for them, I expected to be compensated, and that's where the talks broke down. Still, at least we had civil conversations.

We had more conversations over the winter of 1997-98. I approached the Red Sox Vice President of Marketing, Larry Cancro, with a proposal to publish the team's scorebook/magazine as an independent contractor. Larry heard me out and asked for a detailed proposal, which I gave him. We had a few more chats, and I met with the team's printer, Mass Envelope, but it went nowhere.

The sticking points were my desire to be compensated for the business I was giving up, and their unwillingness to trust me with their official publication. I felt that if I were going to walk away from a lucrative business to work for the Red Sox, then they should either buy out my business or give me a long-term contract.

From their perspective, I suppose they were uncomfortable handing over their official publication, a magazine that reflected directly on them, to someone they didn't know or trust. I had been a vocal critic of the team and a direct competitor, and many of the Red Sox employees I had made to look foolish were still working at Fenway Park.

At any rate, the team would not or could not pull the trigger, and it was back to business as usual in the spring.

Mike Gimbel took over as a regular columnist, replacing Mark Scapicchio, who was taking a one-year sabbatical to focus on (ahem) revenue-related activities.

We dropped the box scores, which we had started running just the year before. They were time-consuming to format and they took up a lot of space, and nobody seemed to care one way or another if we ran them, so we stopped.

One feature we kept that everyone loved — everyone except the Sox and their players, that is — was listing the players' salaries on the roster sheet.

While the *Globe* and *Herald* report contract figures and salary negotiations, neither paper regularly prints the player's salaries. Nowadays,
when salaries are so high and a player's contract status is as important as
his bat or glove, how can you not publish them right there with the batting averages and ERAs?

The season began with great anticipation. "Boston appears closer to
winning that long-awaited World Championship than at any time in the
last two decades," I wrote in April.

Pedro did not disappoint, winning 19 games and posting a 2.89
ERA. However, the Yankees were peaking; they won 114 games and ran
away with the division. The Red Sox made the playoffs as the wild card,
but were beaten by the Indians in the first round.

*Boston Baseball* set new records for both ballpark sales (up 23%) and
ad sales. Late in the season, we sold our one millionth magazine. It was a
staggering figure given the crude newsletter we had started out with nine
years earlier. That one millionth copy was sold by veteran hawker Tim
Dineen to Paul Dunn of New Jersey, who won a trip to the Red Sox
Fantasy Camp.

We had an interesting crew in those years. Sly left in 1998 to join
the Marines and we relied on a mixture of old and new guys to get the
magazines sold.

John was still around, but he was no longer a chunky Irish kid from
Charleston, a classic Boston stereotype. John announced that he was gay,
first to me, then to all the guys, an announcement so unexpected that
nobody could believe, for a while, that it wasn't a big joke.

Being the funny bastard that he was, those were interesting times.
Some of the hawkers, notably Sly, had a hard time with it. He'd hit John
with every slur he could think of, and John would come right back at
him with one-liners that would make Sly squirm.

John changed his life and his lifestyle, losing a lot of weight and
hanging out with a different crowd. Coming out may have been liberat-
ing, but his new friends did him in. The last time I saw John he had gotten into trouble. He borrowed money from me, came in a few times to
try to work it off, and then disappeared completely. He's been sighted
around the ballpark once or twice since then, so he's still around somewhere.

Another one of our top hawkers back then was Johan. He had a very different style from our other successful hawkers; he was quiet and persistent rather than loud and flamboyant.

Johan brought in his friend Mike, and Mike brought in his brother and another friend, so those guys made up about half the crew. Lemon and Sly were convinced that they were all gay, and I suspect that was true, but I didn't care. They were good sellers and they were reliable.

Ben was a student at Emerson. It was generally assumed that Ben spent his *Boston Baseball* earnings on pot, which was also fine with me as long as he didn't smoke it on the premises. I can't say I ever saw Ben smoke a joint, but I do remember Ben coming in early one day and laying down on the cement floor to take a nap before work.

Lemon and Hai also thought that Ben's smoking was fine, because as runners they made a percentage of sales, and they were convinced that Ben was a better hawker stoned than straight.

Ben wanted to write a screenplay about *Boston Baseball*, and we talked it over many times. It was going to be *Taxi* except at the ballpark instead of a cab company, with me in the cage instead of Danny DeVito.

Later Ben set his sights on stand-up comedy, and we ran ads for his gigs in Boston. Ben was another funny guy — we were blessed with several of them. But while he could always crack us up ragging on one of the hawkers, his standup routines were not as good.

Dave Devlin was an older guy, tall and wild-haired, who liked Keno, was a chain smoker, and was down to his last few teeth. Dave was having tough times when he came to work for us, living in a shelter, but he turned himself around.

There was no harm in him, but he liked to scare Lemon. If Lemon as the runner ever let Dave run out of books, Dave would come back to the garage yelling "Lemon? Lemon! Where is that little %$#@^&* Lemon?!"

Ben Boime

Albert hawking from his motorized chair

The crowds at Fenway Park were overwhelmingly white in those days, and so were the hawkers, both inside and out. We were blessed one year with a trio of black kids who showed up to work together and did great things for us.

I always told the hawkers that the more they looked like a ballplayer, the more magazines they would sell. Robinson proved that. Truth is, he was a football player and not a baseball player, but boy, could he sell. His friend Kevaughn was almost as good, and the third kid, T, was no slouch either. Robinson ended up playing college football at Plymouth State, and we still see Kevaughn at the ballpark from time to time.

We had some older hawkers, too. Albert was a World War Two veteran confined to an electric wheelchair. We'd put him at one of the quieter gates, and although he didn't set any sales records, he was thankful for the work, for the money, and for something to do. Each winter he would write me a letter in his shaky handwriting, thanking me for the opportunity and expressing his hope that he'd be able to return the next year. After three years we didn't see him any more.

And then there was Jimmy, an older guy down on his luck. He was working as a waiter or caterer and often went out to sell wearing his red *Boston Baseball* t-shirt over a white dress shirt, tuxedo pants, and shiny black shoes. He had a terrific-sounding British accent and liked to suggest that he was used to better things.

But he was a drinker, and drinking clashed with his medications. One day he collapsed while selling outside the ballpark, and they took him away in an ambulance. He did make a comeback, but it didn't last long.

That's not to say that all our hawkers were troubled kids or down-and-out drunks. Most of them were high school and college kids who worked a year or two, had a great time, made some money, laughed along with the regular hawkers, and moved on. That's the way it should be, because hawking magazines is not a job you build your life around.

The big news of 1998 was the proposal to build a new Fenway Park across the street from the existing one.

The Yawkey Trust, headed by John Harrington, announced that Fenway Park was decrepit and obsolete. Any renovation or expansion, they argued, would be either physically impossible or financially ruinous. The team proposed that the façade of the old ballpark be retained, but that the rest of it be torn down and that a new, bigger Fenway Park be built across the street in the triangle formed by Brookline Avenue and Boylston Street.

There were several problems with this proposal, and no shortage of folks willing to point them out. First, not everyone was willing to give up on the old Fenway Park or to concede that the structure was no longer viable. Second, the Red Sox did not own the land they hoped to build on — they were looking to the City to take it by eminent domain. Third, the neighborhood was not enthused about the plan.

Finally, the Yawkey Trust couldn't fund such an large project by themselves. They were asking for major assistance from the City and the Commonwealth, such as had been received by other professional teams around the country. They would also have needed to borrow large sums to fund their own contribution to the project.

Given that the stock market had doubled from 1994 to 1998, the Yawkey Trust doubtless thought that the timing was right. However, nothing happens quickly in Boston, and the project immediately became embroiled in contentious debate.

Interestingly, there were plenty of folks who were willing to bid adieu to the "lyric little ballpark" as John Updike had called it. Most of them, I suspect, were taller than six feet or over 200 pounds. Others banded together to form a group called Save Fenway Park and lobbied aggressively to keep the Sox in their ancestral home.

*Boston Baseball* offered mixed reviews of the plan. Some of our columnists were ready to move on. Personally, I loved the old ballpark, and was anxious about what a change might mean for my business. A bigger ballpark would mean more fans and more sales. But a new ballpark in the suburbs might be surrounded by team-owned land that I would be barred from.

I was sympathetic to the Save Fenway folks. They were my kind of people. I printed their press releases and ran their ads. Privately, however, I suspected that the old park was doomed, and that my wisest course was not to go down fighting the new park, but rather to focus on the debate over what that new park would be like.

This went on for over a year, until the economy softened and the Yawkey Trust was worn out. Fenway Park survived, and attention was refocused not on its allegedly crumbling foundations, but on the Yawkey Trust. Could the team be operated indefinitely by the executors of the long-dead Yawkeys? Would that be good thing for anyone, apart from John Harrington?

Maybe it was time for new blood.

Members of the group 'Save Fenway Park' collect signatures on Lansdowne Street

Again I met with Larry Cancro over the offseason, and again we could not come to terms. I offered to forego a buyout or a contract and work on a year-to-year basis, but the Red Sox would not pull the trigger.

No matter. 1999 was another banner season for *Boston Baseball*. We eclipsed our old sales record despite the fact that Sly was on active duty with the Marines and would miss the next three full seasons — a parallel to the career of his hero, Ted Williams.

The new top gun was Ryan Goldney, a kid from Revere with a passing resemblance to Nomar Garciaparra.

Ryan won 14 of the next 18 homestands before moving on to full-time employment. He has continued to be a weekend warrior for us to the present day, however, and he hasn't lost his touch at all.

Back then, our hawkers would regularly be given extra tickets to games. Whenever that happened, they'd race back to the garage at count-out time, tear off their *Boston Baseball* t-shirt, and rush back up the street to sell them to the highest bidder.

Taking off the shirt was key. During the first few years of *Boston Baseball*, when the team was bad and tickets were plentiful, I had to step in to stop hawkers from selling tickets while they were working. Scalping was prevalent, but it was also illegal, and I didn't want my hawkers to get a bad reputation with the Boston Police. I issued strict orders that nobody was to buy or sell tickets on the job. If they got tickets they wanted to sell, they needed to come inside and take off their *Boston Baseball* gear first.

Imagine my embarrassment, then, when that summer I was arrested myself for trying sell some extra tickets.

I had acquired four great field box seats with the intention of going with friends. But my plans had fallen through and now, on the day of the game, I realized I wasn't going to be able to use them. I knew perfectly well where the scalpers were to be found. It's the same guys on the same corner, day after day and year after year. So on my way back from the Store 24 in Kenmore Square, where I had gone to buy a case of water for the hawkers, I walked up and offered my tickets.

The scalpers wouldn't give me what they were worth — it was day game in July, a sure sellout, and they were great seats — so I put the tickets back in my wallet, hoisted the case of water onto my shoulder, and headed back to the garage.

I had gone two blocks when one of the scalpers came running up behind me and said he'd buy the tickets at my price. I put down the case of water and produced the tickets. The scalper sprinted off, an undercover cop tapped me on the shoulder, and I was under arrest. The scalper had tipped the cops off so they could make an arrest and leave him and the rest of the pros alone.

A uniformed officer took the tickets and handcuffed me. A squad car came up and they stuffed me in the back, with the windows rolled up on a hot day in July. The cops didn't know what to do with my case of water, and they graciously agreed to drop it off at my office. The squad car pulled up, they dropped off the water, the hawkers gaped, and off we went to the police station.

After twenty minutes of sweating in the back seat, sitting on my own handcuffed hands, I was deposited at the station. They took my wallet and my belt (in case I was inclined to hang myself) and locked me up for an hour before letting me bail myself out. I was back at the park in time to count out the hawkers, who were hugely amused, and remain so to this day.

I had to go court later that summer, where my case was dismissed

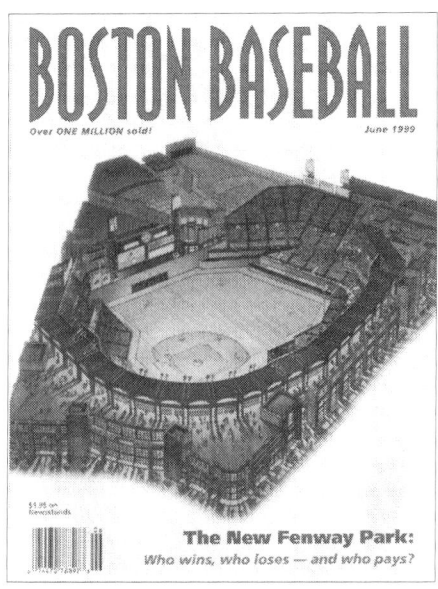

June, 1999

July, 1999

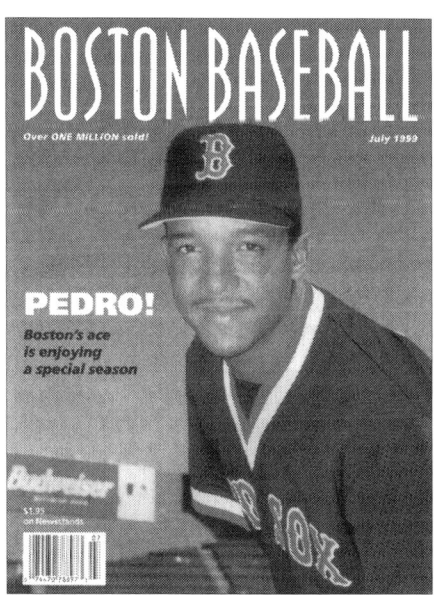

after I had paid court costs. My four prime tickets were never seen again. Photocopies of the tickets were produced as evidence at the hearing, but who ended up in those seats?

The next year, the same thing happened to a veterinarian from Canton. He was so irate he refused to pay court costs and his case went to trial. In the end, the City decided that in the future they would only look to arrest those engaged in the *business* of buying and selling tickets.

Far from being a victory for the average Joe, this decision backfired horribly. Rather than try to distinguish who was and who wasn't in the *business* of scalping tickets, the police backed off completely and the streets around Fenway Park became a scalping free-for-all. More than once I've seen rival scalpers come to blows right outside Fenway Park and beat each other to a pulp.

Ten years later, it's still the same guys on the same corner, day after day and year after year. Everyone around the ballpark knows who they are, including the Boston Police Department. But they're still there.

There were other interesting stories in 1999 besides my arrest. Before the season even started, the Red Sox had tried to rid themselves of the street vendors by refusing to renew their permits.

After being blasted by the media (my own contribution being a column entitled "The World Champs of Hypocrisy") and implored by the City, the Red Sox backed down and renewed the permits. There were some changes on Yawkey Way, however. The decision was made to close the street to traffic on game days, which was long overdue. Some vendors were shuffled around, but overall the closure of the street worked well.

On the field, the Red Sox enjoyed a strong season. Pedro Martinez was brilliant, and the pitching staff allowed the fewest runs in the league. Boston won 94 games, finishing second to the Yankees and returning to the postseason for the third time in five years.

The Red Sox beat Cleveland in the Division Series; anyone who watched the deciding Game Five remembers it well. Twice the Indians walked Garciaparra rather than pitch to him with men on base; twice Troy O'Leary followed with home runs. When Bret Saberhagen couldn't hold back the Tribe, the ailing Pedro Martinez came on and tossed six hitless innings of relief.

In the ALCS against the Yankees, the Sox dropped the first two games in New York by one-run margins and eventually lost in five. But the ancient rivalry, which had been renewed earlier that year when Roger Clemens donned pinstripes, was now fully reignited.

Our All-Star magazine

This was also the year that the All-Star Game returned to Boston after a 38-year hiatus.

I wanted to produce a special magazine for the All-Star Game, but doing so required a fairly large investment, and I was afraid that we'd get to the all-star break and it would rain. Eventually I decided to go ahead with a glossy, full-color, perfect-bound magazine that was the most ambitious publication I had yet produced. It sold for $5.

Rather than wait until the event itself, I printed the All-Star magazine in April, and each day during the first half of the season the hawkers would take out five or ten copies along with the current issue of *Boston Baseball*. I offered them a nice commission on the All-Star books. In this way, regardless of what the weather was like for the event itself, at least we'd have sold some of what we printed.

When the All Star FanFest opened at the Hynes Convention Center downtown, we stationed hawkers outside on Boylston Street. We worked out of the Sir Speedy across the street — they had been printing our inserts for the past several years — and our sales down there were enough to pay the printing bill.

By the time the All Stars arrived for the Home Run Derby, we were in high gear. The weather held, the crowds came, Ted Williams held forth from his golf cart, and overall, both the event and our magazine were a huge success.

Recently there's been talk about bringing the All-Star Game back for Fenway Park's 100th anniversary in 2012. It can't happen soon enough for me.

We had a strong crew that year. Ryan remained our top guy, averaging well over 400 programs a game. Lemon and Hai stuffed the books, for which I can never thank them enough, and worked as runners. Veterans like Tim, Ben, Johan, and Dave were joined by kids like Joe Morelli and older guys like Bill Clark.

Joe came to us as a fresh-faced high school kid. He started hanging around with the older hawkers — Tim Michaud and his pals introduced Joe to beer, among other things — and pretty soon he had put in eleven years at *Boston Baseball*. He tried to retire after ten years, took a month off, and came back. He likes selling magazines, and he's good it; he just doesn't always get along with Sly.

Joe's quick, he's funny, he can sell programs by the boxload when he wants to, but he's never won a homestand despite being one of our top guys for years. Something always seems to happen. Defeat is snatched from the jaws of victory.

Bill was a different story. I'm not saying Bill was big, but he did well up on the Bridge because folks couldn't squeeze past him without buying a program. Bill would regularly ask Lemon or Hai for help tying his shoes. Bill's arms weren't long enough reach around his stomach and into his apron, so he would invite fans to take their own magazines and make their own change.

Despite his size, he was an effective hawker and even won a homestand that summer, the only homestand Ryan didn't win.

The way Bill told it, he had been a hockey star in high school, but tore up his knee. Once he could no longer play hockey, he put on weight, and so it went until he turned up at *Boston Baseball*. Bill sold for us for a couple of years, and he was a pleasure to have around.

He left suddenly, however, because he had gotten in deep with one of the bookies around the ballpark. One week he won $4,000; the next week he lost it all, including another $1,000 that he didn't have. Threats were made, and quickly Bill was headed for Alabama, never to be seen again.

*Boston Baseball* featured some inspired writing in 1999. Much of it was dedicated to the ongoing debate over the future of Fenway Park, but columnist Mark Scapicchio also deserves a shout-out; in our All-Star Magazine, he suggested that the winner of the All-Star Game should earn home-field advantage in the World Series, a suggestion that MLB adopted in 2003.

This was also the summer of our most popular feature ever. "The Emperor has No Clothes" was a series of six articles by Doug Pappas on Boston's unusual ownership situation. The series asked "How did an accountant who never invested a dime of his own money in the Sox become the absolute boss of New England's most storied sports franchise? What are the implications for Harrington's unaccountable authority for the Sox, their fans, Fenway Park, and Major League Baseball?"

This was the most discussed piece of journalism we had ever published to that point. I got more comments and more compliments on that series than on anything else in the magazine. Doug had been, to that point, just one of our stable of interesting contributors, but that year he became one of our stars. Anything by Doug — and he continued to pen his regular column while working on "The Emperor has No

Clothes"— became a must-read.

Before the '99 season was over, he and I had already agreed to follow up with a similar series in 2000, devoted to the new stadiums that had grown up around baseball, how they had been financed, and whether they had delivered the promised benefits to the municipalities that helped build them.

Big Bill Clark

105

Lemon, Mike, and Hai working the 1999 All Star Game at Fenway Park

Although sales had continued to grow, my ambition to make the magazine bigger and better with each issue came with a price. The magazine was becoming more and more expensive to produce, while we were still selling it for the same $1 price we had started with ten years earlier.

Clearly, I had to make a decision. I could hold the line at $1 and accept some limitations on what the magazine could be, or I could raise the price.

Raising the price seems like the obvious answer, but remember, we were selling this magazine on the street. Having a price that wasn't an even-dollar amount was going to complicate our operations enormously. If we went to $1.50, for example, and averaged 2,000 books a game and everyone either gave or needed change, we'd be counting out 4,000 quarters a day — one hundred rolls of quarters! We'd be starting earlier, finishing later, and every transaction would take more time.

It was a lot simpler to hold the line, and that's why I continued to do so even after the magazine had grown and changed dramatically. I looked to advertising revenues to help pay for my increasing production costs, but the big-name advertisers, the national chains and national products, were opting for the glossy, full-cover Red Sox magazine — even though they were paying three or four times as much per reader.

By 2000, I felt I could justify a price increase, even a 100% price increase, because the magazine was obviously a better product and a better value than it had been in 1990. The increase would allow us to produce a glossy magazine, most of it in color. For the first time, our production values could rival those of the official publication. The competition for advertisers would then take place on a more level playing field.

It wasn't an easy decision. I knew that the $1 price was appealing, and that we would lose some readers. But how many? Would we lose 20%, 30%, 40%? The Red Sox had long ago raised their price back to $2, $2.50, and then $3, so we'd still be significantly less expensive than the official scorebook.

Finally I decided that there was no sense staying where I was and getting squeezed. I would raise the price, go to a glossy format, and trust that our readers would stick with us. The April issue, bearing our 10th

Anniversary logo, sold for $1, but announced the new price of $2 beginning in May.

I cut up one of our magazine boxes to make a presentation board. On it, I showed the hawkers what they were making now, with the magazine $1, and the higher commission they make when we went to $2. I also showed them what would happen to their take-home wages at different sales levels — if we lost 20%, 30%, 40% of our volume. I told them that yes, we would lose some readers. But unless we lost a lot more than I expected, both the hawkers and I would end up with more money in our pockets. We'd also have a better-looking magazine to sell, a magazine that could continue to grow and improve.

The first month was the hardest. Fans who had become accustomed to walking up to our hawkers with a dollar bill at the ready would have to be told that sorry, the price was now $2. Would they walk away, or would they dig out another dollar?

It was May, of course — a tough month under any circumstances — but still, the initial returns were disturbing. We'd averaged 2,100 magazines a game in 1999. In May of 2000, selling our first $2 issue, we averaged under 1,000. It was our worst month in eight years.

Suspecting that I had made a terrible mistake, I put a good face on it and stuck to my guns. June was better; we averaged 1,200 magazines a

May, 2000 — after ten years
of holding the line at a buck,
we raised the price to $2

The ballpark crew, circa 2000

game. The hawkers got off my back. In July, we averaged nearly 1,800 magazines a game, and we all shared a sigh of relief. *Boston Baseball* would live.

It's a heck of a magazine for $2. I think our readers recognized that, and that's what brought them around. Doug Pappas was back with a season-long series called "The House that YOU Built." What could be more timely than an examination of the return on investment for the taxpayers in Baltimore, Cleveland, and Chicago who had recently built new ballparks?

We also launched a new kind of continuing series. We decided that each year we would choose an important new baseball book and run excerpts from it in each issue. In 2000 and 2001 we ran excerpts from the newly-published history of the club, *Red Sox Century*, by our own Glenn Stout and Dick Johnson.

Given that the book challenged many common perceptions about the club and its history — especially the so-called 'Curse of the Bambino' — it made for great reading. *Red Sox Century* remains the one essential book for any serious fan of the team.

But not all our additions to the editorial were serious and educational. I had always been an avid reader of the funny pages, from

*Doonesbury* to *Calvin & Hobbes* to *Dilbert.* For several years I had been toying with an idea for a baseball comic strip that could run in the magazine. Over that winter I shared my ideas with illustrator Stephen Lloynd, and together we created a strip called *The Scrubs.*

The Scrubs were a Little League team sponsored by Denny's Scrub-a-Dub, a car wash. The strip was peopled with barely-disguised characters. The long-suffering manager, Sheldon, was based on my father, who had the misfortune of coaching me as a Little Leaguer. The team's star was a high-living ten-year-old named Dangerous Dave, based on my friend Dave Colozzi.

The team's star pitcher, Michelle, overshadowed her ineffective sidekick, Zach. These characters were based on former Tufts righty Zach Soolman and his softball-playing girlfriend.

I had a lot of grins putting the strips together. Did anyone else think they were funny? Not really, no. But I hope to revisit the Scrubs some day. Now that I'm a Little League coach myself, I know there's a gold mine of material there.

At the end of the season, when the numbers were all added up, we had seen sales decline by 33%. That was more than I had bargained for. But at $2, we still took in 25% more revenue. As I had predicted to the

Justin

hawkers back in April, we all went home with a little more money in our pockets.

That was saying something, given the lackluster year that the Red Sox had on the field. The Yankees were beatable — they won just 87 games — yet the Sox couldn't catch them. The pitching was great, but the offense struggled despite Nomar's career-high .372 average.

Meanwhile, in Kansas City, Johnny Damon led the league in runs with 136. In Cleveland, Manny Ramirez led the league in slugging. Why couldn't we get players like that?

It didn't hurt that we had a good crew of hawkers that year. Sly was still in the service, and Ryan remained our main man. We picked up a strong new seller in Justin, a student at Northeastern. I gave Justin the Red Sox stirrup socks I had been issued at Fantasy Camp, and he used to wear them while he was selling, with his pants hiked up to his knees.

Justin was another funny and streetwise kid who was not intimidated by Sly or anyone else. He ended up going to New York City to become a police officer.

He was our second policeman after Sly's friend Scott, who worked for us in 1994 before joining the Marines. Scott came back and joined the Special Operations arm of the BPD. We'd see him once in a while on the ballpark detail, but he left the force after being shot in the jaw and the arm in the line of duty.

Coupled with a modest increase in ad sales, we'd had our best year ever in 2000. I thought we had overcome a hurdle. As I would soon realize, we had done much more than that.

The Sox had another so-so season in 2001. On the field, the real action was in the American League West, where the Seattle Mariners won 116 games and Oakland finished second despite winning 102.

The Sox, at 82-79, were 13 games in back of the Yankees. The offense was improved, with the addition of Manny Ramirez. But the pitching fell to earth.

Still, attendance was good. Sales revenues were up. And then there was PSP.

Professional Sports Publications was a company out of New York that specialized in selling print ads for sporting magazines, yearbooks, and programs. In some markets they would publish the programs themselves.

At Boston College, for example, if you went to a football game and bought a program, you were buying a PSP product. PSP produced a generic college football magazine, and then bound in a section that was specific to each customer, in this case BC. It gave the schools a more impressive publication than they would have been able to produce themselves, and both BC and PSP could make money on the advertising.

PSP also sold advertising for many professional sports teams, including the Red Sox. But the teams were less reliant on PSP than the colleges were and the relationships tended to be more contentious. The teams had their own sponsors, whom they wanted to protect. If the Red Sox had an agreement with Coca-Cola, for example, they would inform PSP that competitors such as Pepsi were off limits.

In most major-league cities, that would be the end of it, but in Boston there were two magazines sold at the ballpark. Lou Yaffe, who was PSP's man in Boston, took a look at the newly-glossy *Boston Baseball* and realized that if he couldn't put Pepsi in the Red Sox' book, he could put Pepsi into *Boston Baseball*.

Given that our ad rates were lower than the Sox' rates while our circulation was higher, *Boston Baseball* was an attractive alternative to advertisers, and in PSP we had the ideal partner to push ad sales.

Over our first ten years of publication, we had grown advertising revenues from $1,800 in that first year to about $40,000 in 2000. In

2001, with PSP placing advertisers such as Wendy's, Canon, New York Life, Pioneer, Hyundai, and HBO in the magazine, that figure quadrupled to $160,000.

I was rich!

At least, it felt that way. But I didn't go out and buy a BMW. I gave modest raises to the writers, photographers and hawkers, and continued to grow and improve the publication. The magazine was all color, all glossy now, and as usual we had some fun new features.

Bill Nowlin, the author of several books about the Red Sox, provided us with a series of interviews with folks who worked in and around the ballpark. Eventually published as *Fenway Lives* (Rounder Books, 2004), the book drew on over 200 interviews with players, media, grounds crew, hawkers, vendors, ushers, trainers — you name it. It's the best book I've ever seen when it comes to depicting how business gets done at Fenway Park.

The first interview we published was with Nick Jacobs. Later that year we ran one with P.J. McCaul, who was the manager for Ryan Family Amusements, the bowling alley underneath Fenway. Yes, there used to be a bowling alley under Fenway Park, and in all those years it never occurred to the Yawkey Trust that there might be a better use for that space.

May, 2001

Tony Massarotti did a terrific piece for us on the Red Sox clubhouse. It included a diagram showing where all the player's lockers were. There's always been a lot of talk about the Red Sox clubhouse. Here, for the first time that I'm aware of, was a map of it!

One corner of the clubhouse featured Jose Offerman, Manny Ramirez, and Carl Everett — three lockers right in a row. Wouldn't you have liked to be a fly on that wall?

Although I didn't buy a BMW that summer, I did begin exploring another idea.

My family and I had left town for the North Shore in 1996, opting for a four-bedroom house on the Essex River over a three-bedroom condo in Brookline at the same price. We missed the excitement and diversity of the city, but we hoped to make up for that by pursuing our interest in sailing. In 1998 we bought a small sailboat and docked it in Beverly.

On the waterfront near the marina was a granite marker commemorating the 1775 launching of the armed schooner *Hannah*, called by some America's first naval vessel. I had always been interested in history and in sailing, and I went to the Beverly Public Library to find out more about *Hannah*. Pretty soon, I had drawn up a business plan for building a replica of this historic vessel, which would be based in Beverly and would earn its keep taking the public on two-hour sails.

The project was too big for me to finance by myself, even with the checks from PSP, so I began making the rounds on the North Shore, looking for partners. I wasn't sure where it might lead, but after eleven years at the ballpark, I was definitely interested in a new challenge.

Unfortunately, Tim Michaud was thinking the same thing. Tim had been hawking magazines for me for many years, because he liked the work, he was good at it, and he was not particularly interested in getting a real job, even after he graduated from Emerson College.

Our hawkers have always been alternative people. Given the seasonal, part-time nature of the job, they come and they go. The ones who stick with it year after year generally fall into two categories — those incapable of doing better, and those unwilling to settle down into the drudgery of a regular job.

Tim was one of the latter. He was a bright kid, engaging and funny. I don't think he came from the happiest of backgrounds, but at the ballpark he was usually able to make the best of any situation. If it rained, Tim would make hats out of the magazines and little boats out of dollar bills, which he would float in the gutter.

In 2001 Tim decided that if I could make money with *Boston Baseball*, he could do it too. He launched his own newsletter (titled *6-4-3*, and later *Beantown Baseball*, aka *The Bean*) in an attempt to compete head to head with *Boston Baseball*. He contacted some of my past and current hawkers about jumping ship, and set up shop on the same street corners.

Tim's newsletter was not very good, but having another publication out there was definitely not in my best interest. Remembering how the Red Sox had reacted to my publication a decade earlier, and how that had had devolved into a dozen years of hostility, I resolved to take a different tack. I offered Tim a deal.

If he would agree to sell his newsletter *after* the games instead of before them, he could use my space at the ballpark rent free, and I would run an ad for his newsletter in *Boston Baseball*. If he sold *after* the games, he could use whichever of my hawkers chose to stick around.

Tim accepted my offer, but he had trouble getting his business off the ground. It's tough selling after the games, when it's dark and most people just want to get home. Sales weren't good, and it was hard to persuade hawkers to work for him.

Tim Michaud, Hai Ho Nguyen, Colm Gormley

He responded by printing up clever (and some not-so-clever) bumper stickers that were given out free with every newsletter. People liked the stickers; in fact, they liked them better than the newsletter. Tim's hawkers quickly realized this and stopped promoting the newsletter, instead holding up the stickers.

But stickers by themselves are merchandise. Selling them by themselves required a permit, and permits are not to be had. So Code Enforcement continually gave him a hard time, as it became obvious that the newsletter, which never grew beyond a dozen pages, had become a cover for what was essentially an unlicensed bumper-sticker business.

After about two years of this, Tim called it quits. I was glad to see him go. Code Enforcement was really cracking down on Tim's hawkers, and some of those guys also worked for me. The last thing I need is trouble with Code Enforcement.

But Tim did make one lasting contribution to *Boston Baseball*, the notion that a catchy bumper sticker or other giveaway could dramatically boost sales. It was a tactic we'd make use of in the coming years.

The 2001 season saw one of my favorite advertisers come and go. Jim Dunn, a stand-up comic from New Hampshire, developed a site called DrunkenFan.com.

The site featured a collection of merchandise including caps and t-shirts with a flaming keg logo, as well as baseball uniform shirts with the keg logo on the front, DRUNKEN FAN on the back where the player's name would go, and ".10", the legal limit for intoxication, as the number.

The concept tickled me, so I agreed to run Jim's ads in exchange for merchandise, which I still have today. Sadly, other people didn't find it as amusing as I did, and after a year Jim moved on to other things.

This was the time of the so-called internet bubble. Everyone was rushing to get online. *Eagle Action* had developed a premium website (one that members paid to access) on the Rivals.com network. Anxious to stake their claim beyond college sports, Rivals paid me to develop content for Bruins, Celtics, and Red Sox sites as well.

Within two years, of course, Red Sox sites were legion, some with thousands and others with dozens of adherents. When Rivals went bankrupt and then re-formed a year later, I was happy to shed those three websites and get back to focusing on Boston College.

I get asked all the time why *Boston Baseball* doesn't have a bigger web presence. My response has always been that I would return to the internet when I could make money there. My experience has taught me that periodicals can only make money on the internet if they have valuable, *unique* content — in which case they should charge for it, not give it away.

Many people thought that if you staked out your territory early and built a great website, you could turn a profit by selling advertising. But ten years down the road, that has yet to become true. Ad revenues from the internet don't begin to justify the time and effort required to maintain a top-flight website — especially one devoted to the Red Sox, with an excellent official site and a hundred unofficial competitors, some of them quite good.

August of 2001 marked a watershed for *Boston Baseball*. After years of unflagging support for Red Sox GM Dan Duquette, we abandoned ship.

His free-agent signings had been, by and large, good ones. The core of the 2004 World Champions was already in place. But the ballyhooed transformation of the Red Sox minor-league organization had not occurred. Sure, people lost their jobs, but the drafts under Duquette had not been particularly productive. At the big-league level, after the promise of 1995 and 1998, Duquette had failed to take the Red Sox all the way.

True, the Yawkey Trust ownership, distracted and ineffectual, could have done more to support him. But he was given time, money, and control enough to get the job done, and he didn't. The final straw came when Duquette replaced Jimy Williams with his pal Joe Kerrigan. We washed our hands of the Duke, and looked ahead to the imminent sale of the team and the housecleaning that was sure to follow.

One month later, two hijacked jetliners struck the World Trade Center.

Apart from everything else, the atmosphere at Fenway Park changed overnight. Fans were concerned about attending big public events. Teams rushed to put security precautions in place. Confused lines developed outside the turnstiles as newly-hired guards frisked fans and searched handbags. Larger bookbags and knapsacks were banned altogether.

Leave it to Lemon and Hai to find an opportunity in this mess. Piles of discarded backpacks were forming outside each gate as fans, turned away by security, discovered that there was no place to check their bags. They emptied them of valuables, added their bags to the pile, and went to the game.

Once Lemon and Hai were done working for me, they would return to the piles, pick through them for the nicest backpacks, clean them up, and sell them through Craig's List or on eBay.

Lemon paid for his opportunism, however. One of the backpacks he kept, and he brought it with him on a trip to Australia. Passing through customs, a drug-sniffing dog caught a whiff of something on the bag, and Lemon had to talk his way out of a potentially bad situation.

It was a pretty grim September, but it ended with a bang as Cal Ripken Jr. and the Orioles came to town for his last appearance at Fenway Park.

Ripken had packed the ballpark in 1995 when he was chasing Lou Gehrig's consecutive-games record, and we expected it would be a big event. Our colleagues down in Baltimore had printed up a special commemorative issue of *Outside Pitch*, and they asked if I wanted to try selling it outside Fenway while the Orioles were in town. I agreed, and their magazine sold even better than I had expected.

In fact, they sold so well that the hawkers stopped pushing *Boston Baseball* — the Red Sox having been eliminated weeks earlier — and focused on the Ripken magazine. I had given them a generous commission on the Ripken magazines, and they quickly figured out where their best interests lay.

It was a four-game series and we'd sold all the magazines after two games. I called the guys in Baltimore and asked if they had any more. They threw some boxes on the northbound Amtrak, the magazines arrived at South Station that evening, and we sold them at Fenway for the regular-season finale.

Septembers can be rough on the hawkers, especially when the team has been eliminated, so it was nice they had a few decent paydays at the end of the season.

The Red Sox ended that year with a long roadtrip. When it was finally over, I got a call from the guys in Baltimore. I had already sent them the money for the magazines, but they decided they wanted a different deal, a bigger cut than we had originally agreed on for the first batch of magazines.

I told them that if they had wanted to change the deal, then they should have said so before they sent me the second batch of magazines. As it was, the magazines were sold, the commissions were paid, and I had given them what I had originally agreed to give them.

Maybe they had run out of magazines at the end of the season in Baltimore and regretted having sent me that second shipment. At any rate, I refused to send them any more money, and they haven't spoken to me since. They even took me off their mailing list.

Money changes everything, as Cyndi Lauper once said.

And on that note, let me say one more thing about the 2001 season: the average seat at Fenway cost $36, up 250% since 1991.

By 2009, the only place you could sit for $36 was in the bleachers.

Over the winter, Lucky John Harrington and the Yawkey Trust finally slunk off the stage.

In a move that dovetailed a little too neatly with Major League Baseball's plans for the Montreal and Florida franchises, Harrington passed on two higher bids and sold to a group headed by former Marlins owner John Henry. Pointed questions about the sale being on the level from Massachusetts Attorney General Tom Reilly prompted the new owners to kick in some additional money and make a commitment to charitable giving.

It was immediately apparent that the new ownership was younger, smarter, and more capable than their predecessors. It was also apparent that having paid over $700 million for the Red Sox and NESN, they were determined to recoup their investment as soon as possible.

On the plus side, changes that had been crying out to be made for decades — both on and off the field — were finally made. The entire organization was flushed out. The rugs were beaten, the closets cleaned, the attic aired. Doors that had been bricked over and windows that had painted shut were opened once more. Dumpster after dumpster was filled with nepotism and incompetence and hauled off to the landfill.

Encouraged by this new spirit, I dusted off my last, best proposal to the Red Sox and resubmitted it. I received no answer. My introduction to the new owners wouldn't come for a few more months, by which time I would have an entirely different feeling about the changes on Yawkey Way.

Sly was back in 2002 after missing most of the previous three seasons. The majority of that time he was overseas with his unit, but for some of it he may have been suspended. I've suspended him so many times I can't remember them all. Sly likes to tell newcomers to *Boston Baseball* that he's spent more time on suspension than they've put in at the ballpark.

It's always good when you can put an all-star back in the lineup, but Sly quickly targeted Ryan, who had become the top seller in his absence.

One afternoon when we were counting out, my two top hawkers

started talking smack to each other and suddenly Sly put down the bills he was counting and leaped at Ryan, punching him in the head and knocking him sideways into a stack of boxes. I jumped in, trying to keep them apart, and we all went down in a pile of arms, legs, boxes, magazines and money.

Not for the first time, I had to explain to Sly no matter how many magazines he's sold, no matter how much passion he brings to the ballpark, no matter how charming he can be when he's in a good mood, those positives don't automatically outweigh his negatives — that he's moody, violent and intolerant.

Those were troubling qualities when he was a skinny, hyperactive teenager from East Boston. They were even more troubling now that he was a Marine.

Speaking of which, one day when he was upset at me about something, he walked in during count-out, took a grenade out of his pocket, dropped it in the middle of the office, and ran out.

Everyone froze for a second and then ran out after him. I was trapped behind my desk; there was no way I was going to get out before the grenade went off. I was pretty sure it was a paintball grenade anyway. I ducked behind the desk, and BANG! It exploded.

It was a concussion grenade — loud, but harmless. I stood up and went back to counting, and there I was when the hawkers began trickling back in. From this incident I got a reputation for *sang froid* that I don't deserve, but that's all right. It comes in handy.

In May, with the team playing well and magazines selling briskly, I got a rude awakening. The Red Sox and the City of Boston announced a plan to privatize the entire block in front of Fenway Park on game days.

The Red Sox would be allowed to set up turnstiles at either end of Yawkey Way, barring anyone who did not have a ticket to the game, and blocking access to the businesses across the street — Twin Enterprises and their tenants, such as Who's On First and Best Sausage.

Where once there was a public street, the Red Sox would now roll out a huge new concourse, featuring their own food and beer vendors, souvenir carts, and strolling entertainers. And the vendors who worked on Yawkey Way, some of them for generations? Banished to the far side of the park.

The Red Sox had been scheming for years to control more of the revenues generated by those attending games, from parking to programs to sausages. But now the City was playing along. Mayor Menino was determined to stay on the good side of the wealthy newcomers.

Downtown ballparks have their charms, but for team owners, they also have one significant drawback: some of the revenue generated on game days ends up in other hands than theirs. People park in private lots, they grab a bite at a restaurant before heading into the park, they drop some money in the souvenir store across the street, they pick up a program or a sausage or a bag of peanuts from an independent vendor. None of that money goes to the Red Sox!

At a suburban ballpark, such as Gillette Stadium, a much larger percentage of the money spent goes to the team. The team controls the parking lots, and once you step out of your car, you're on team-owned or team-leased property, and part of every dollar you spend — on parking, food, drinks, or souvenirs — goes into the team's pockets.

The Red Sox have long wished to have their cake and to eat it, too — to enjoy the atmosphere of a downtown park while controlling as much of the revenue as possible. The privatization of Yawkey Way was a big step in that direction.

Why Twins Enterprises agreed to the street closure has never been publicly explained. Twins is more than just the Souvenir Store across from Fenway Park; they are a major provider of licensed souvenirs and sportswear to teams all over the country. They're a privately-held compa-

Kevin

Lemon

ny with over $100 million in annual sales. Did the Sox offer them concession rights in the ballpark? Did Major League Baseball lean on them over licensing? The rumor was that the aged Arthur D'Angelo, who founded the company with his brother, didn't like it, but felt he had no choice.

The Sox and the City announced that there would be a trial of the street closure in September, and if all went smoothly, that the street would be closed off for all future Red Sox games beginning in April of 2003.

For those of us who did business on Yawkey Way, this news was electrifying. As soon as I heard of the proposal, I went to each of the vendors on Yawkey Way — sellers of sunglasses, baseball cards, sausages, peanuts, hats — and urged them to fight it.

I was no lawyer, but I was pretty sure that the process of closing the street would have to be a public one, and that we would get a chance to have our say. Wasn't Yawkey Way a public street? Hadn't independent vendors been working that street since the ballpark opened in 1912? What right did the Red Sox and the City have to relocate us just so the team could make more money?

The vendors were paralyzed. Nobody liked the plan and nobody wanted to move, but they're all dependent on the Red Sox to sign their

Jake Rutstein helps get the word out about
the impending privatization of Yawkey Way

permits each year. None of them dared to say or do anything that might give the team a reason not to renew their permit. Nobody believed that if they did confront the Red Sox, and if permits did become an issue, the Mayor would come to their rescue as he had a few years earlier.

I did discover that the Red Sox were going to host an "informational meeting" for the vendors, and although I wasn't invited, I was determined to attend.

The meeting was scheduled for the morning before a day game. The vendors assembled outside the door to the Red Sox offices next to the ticket office, and at the appointed hour, we headed inside and up the stairs. We milled around in the lobby for a few moments before being invited down a long corridor.

Down the hall we went, me bringing up the rear, until we came to a suite of offices. Suddenly, from a space to my left, Larry Lucchino himself swooped in, took me by the arm, and hustled me alone into an empty office.

The rest of the vendors trooped onward, and Lucchino and I were face to face. I had never met him before.

"This meeting is for the vendors," Lucchino told me, "Not for the media."

"I am a vendor," I insisted. "I've been working on that street for 13 years."

"Yes," Lucchino said, eyeing me. "But this meeting is for the vendors, and they're waiting for me right now. Why don't we set up a separate meeting, just for you, where we can show you what we have in mind?"

I didn't have a choice. He still had me by the arm, and I clearly wasn't going to that meeting. I agreed to call him the next day to set up a private appointment, expecting that when I called, I'd be put off.

But we did have that meeting. Lucchino again was there himself, and he took pains to explain the team's plan for Yawkey Way, how important it was for the team, how he planned to encourage fans to keep using the other gates, and that he felt the impact on the vendors would be minimal.

I thanked him for taking the time to met with me, but I also told him I was convinced that the closure would be disastrous for my business and for the other vendors, that I planned to fight it with as many of the other vendors as I could convince to join me, in court if necessary.

And that was my introduction to the new Red Sox ownership.

I went to Century Type and made up protest signs:

**KEEP YAWKEY WAY A PUBLIC WAY**

**SAY IT AIN'T SO, MAYOR MENINO**

**TODAY'S GAME:**
**Out-of-State Millionaires**
**vs Small Local Businesses**

**NO TURNSTILES**

Every day before we began selling, the hawkers and I would shoulder the signs, parade up and down Yawkey Way, and head back to the office.

My June column urged fans to call Mayor Menino and protest his support of the plan. I argued that the independent vendors were part of the tradition and atmosphere of Fenway Park. More important, creating this huge new concourse for the Red Sox and relocating the vendors would be tantamount to giving the Red Sox a monopoly at the ballpark — a monopoly on sausages, sodas, peanuts, programs, and souvenirs.

Whenever there's a monopoly, it's the consumers who suffer. With their competition banished to the back side of the ballpark, there would be less incentive for the Red Sox and their concessionaire, Aramark, to provide a variety of products at reasonable prices. If the street were closed, I predicted that the already-high prices inside the park would go up even more.

In June, the Sox announced that they had reached an agreement with the vendors over Yawkey Way. My July column likened the "agreement" to a mugging. In truth, the vendors hated the plan, but the Sox held all the cards, and the vendors failed to present a united front. The team excluded me from the talks, divided the vendors, and conquered them.

Under the terms of the agreement, the Sox would get Yawkey Way and the vendors would get to keep their licenses. Remember the sales contest in *Glengarry Glen Ross*? First prize is a Cadillac El Dorado, second prize is a set of steak knives, third prize is you're fired. The Red Sox came in first with this agreement, while the vendors were lucky to keep their businesses.

A few vendors would be allowed to remain at the extreme ends of the street, while the rest would be moved to other gates. The Red Sox promised to make an effort to redirect fans to those other gates, but why would they make over Yawkey Way and then encourage fans to enter at another gate? It made no sense.

The unequal agreement between the Red Sox and the vendors didn't mean I couldn't continue the fight. I began putting out feelers to local law firms as well as national non-profits such as the Conservation Law Foundation and the American Civil Liberties Union to see if there were any legal remedies we could pursue.

Uncertainty over Yawkey Way tended to blind me to the fact that 2002 was a banner year. The team was headed for 93 wins. Derek Lowe moved back into the rotation, going from 20 saves to 20 wins and tossing the first no-hitter at Fenway since 1965.

We set new records for magazine sales and for ad sales. We had some great articles, including a provocative excerpt from Howard Bryant's book *Shut Out: A Story of Race and Baseball in Boston*, in which Jim Rice spoke openly about his experiences with the Red Sox.

Sadly, on July 5, Ted Williams passed away. The Red Sox happened to be home at the time, and although there was no time to put together a special issue, I wanted to mark Ted's passing in some way.

I went to Sir Speedy, who was printing our inserts at the time, and gave them the design for a 4" x 6" card edged in black with a photo of Williams in his prime and the words "Ted Williams: The Splendid Splinter 1918-2002".

We gave the cards away with the magazines the next day and had a huge day, selling over 3,600 magazines at $2. Sly sold 565 magazines by himself and Ryan, Ben, and Joe all sold over 400. We took in over $7,200 that afternoon and I paid out $1,200 in commissions and bonuses.

The Red Sox announced a special memorial service at Fenway Park for July 22. With that much lead time, we were able to put together a special 16-page issue full of stories and photos of Williams, which we sold for $5 before and after the service.

One dollar from every sale went to the Make-A-Wish Foundation — we figured the Jimmy Fund would already have their hands full. The next week we presented a check to Julie Abel of Make-a-Wish for $3,400.

The card we gave away
the day after Teddy Ballgame
died

**Ted Williams**
*"The Splendid Splinter"*
**August 30, 1918 - July 5, 2002**

Just a few days before the service at Fenway, the Licensing Board held a hearing at City Hall on the proposed Yawkey Way concourse. The hearing was held not as a referendum on the seizure of Yawkey Way — no such hearing was ever held — but merely to determine if the Red Sox should be allowed to sell beer there.

Nevertheless, after a statement by the Red Sox touting their agreement with the vendors and claiming that negotiations for privatizing Yawkey Way "were in the bottom of the ninth inning" a number of the scheme's opponents seized the opportunity to speak out.

City Councilor Maura Hennigan spoke in defense of the independent vendors outside the ballpark. Peter Catalano of the Fenway Action Coalition decried the impact of the plan on the neighborhood. I also stood up, introducing myself as the largest employer on the street and someone who had been commended by the City for giving summer job opportunities to Boston youths.

I pointed out that I although I had as much to lose as any of the vendors, I'd been shut out of the negotiations between the Red Sox and the vendors. I argued that the "agreement" between the team and the vendors had essentially been dictated by the Sox, who held the ultimate trump card of being able to refuse to sign the vendors' permits.

I was seconded by an attorney representing Who's on First, a bar that leased space on Yawkey Way from Twins Enterprises. He denied that the team had ever met with his client, prompting the Licensing Board to request that the Red Sox produce documentation of their meetings with local businesses.

Sadly, that was far as we got. The rest of the process went on behind closed doors. The Sox got their permit, and the countdown to September 5 — the first day the Red Sox would be allowed to seal off Yawkey Way with their turnstiles — began.

But as the season wound down, there was something new to worry about: with negotiations over a new agreement between the owners and the players stalled, it appeared that there could be a strike before the end of the regular season.

On August 28, I brought a video camera to work, planning to film the streets around the ballpark as they were in the last days before the privatization took effect. I was also concerned that if there were indeed another strike, the privatization might not matter after all. Interest in Major League Baseball might wither to the point where the magazine was no longer viable, regardless of where we could and couldn't sell it.

Presenting a check to Julie Abel of Make-a-Wish for $3400.
From left: Anthony, Hai, Sly, John, Mike, Joe, Tim, Ryan and Julie

Once the hawkers and runners were on the street, I walked down to Kenmore Square and turned on the camera. I kept filming as I walked with the crowd over the bridge, filming the hawkers at the Bridge and the Cask, the enormous handgun billboard, the Coke bottles that had been installed on the left-field light tower.

There were Boston *Globe* hawkers handing out free newspapers, WEEI interns passing out 'K' cards, street people pawing though the trash for returnable bottles and cans.

There was Nick Jacobs out in front of Gate A, at the spot where his father and grandfather had worked since 1912. There were Twins' green-painted souvenir carts festooned with Dominican flags in honor of Pedro Martinez.

All along Yawkey Way, there were vendors and hawkers doing business. Peanut vendors, sausage carts, hats, caps, and souvenirs, sunglasses, baseball cards. There were my guys: Chris, Anthony, Sly, Ryan, and John, with Lemon pushing the dolly around and around the park. There was Joe Morelli selling outside Gate A, wearing a STRIKES SUCK t-shirt.

It was never going to look like this again.

After the game began and we were all counted out, we were in a nostalgic mood. This was our 13th year at the Fenway Park and some of the guys there had been working for me for six, eight, ten years. That's a

Joe Morelli

Ryan Goldney

long time when you're in your twenties.

I set up the camera on a tripod and asked if any of the guys wanted to talk about their experiences at *Boston Baseball.*

Sly was the first to take me up on it.

"I'm Sly, I'm the MVP, I'm better than everyone," he began, laughing.

He told the story of how he had walked up to me on Yawkey Way and asked me for a job, ten years earlier. He claimed he could even remember the cover of the issue we were selling that day — a Tyler Bolden photo of Mo Vaughn and Fred Thomas standing back to back.

Sly claimed that he sold 300 magazines his first day on the job, then reduced the claim to "250 or 300" (I looked it up; it was 121).

"There were a lot of guerrilla-type guys working here, back in the day," Sly said. "Older guys, guys with facial hair, who went out and drank beer after the game. It was like the Gashouse Gang.

"I must have sold a million magazines here... yeah, a million magazines. I'll probably work here until Mike dies, and then I'll sell the company for liquor and strippers."

Ryan was next.

"I remember the first day I worked here, Mike had me walking Yawkey Way and I broke the record. I sold 130 magazines or whatever and I broke the record and I came in and I was all happy…

"My fondest memory working down here as that first Atlanta series. I was on the bridge and it was a madhouse, I've never seen anything like it in my life, I came back in to the office and there were empty boxes everywhere. It looked like a tornado went through here. I was looking for another box of books so I could go out there!

"I remember Hai and Lemon running around in their rice-paddy hats…"

Sly and Ryan had been around long enough to remember going head-to-head with the Red Sox on the street corners, and they reminisced about what that had been like. These were their war stories, told with pride.

"I basically came in here when the struggle was over," admitted Joe Morelli, "so everything was easy for me. I was reading the newspaper one day in high school — OK, OK, I was in detention! — and I saw an ad for the job in the paper. I had no idea what a hawker was, but I figured OK, I'll try this. I gave Mike a call and he put me out there. My first day I went to the parking lot and broke the record.

"Every year I've been here I've screwed up, and Mike would say 'get the fuck out of here' but I kept coming back…"

"Then there was the time Sly beat up Jeff Brink on the bridge. I was working behind Jeff at the Cask, and Sly came running up because Jeff had been yelling at him about something. Sly came running up to him on the bridge and Jeff grabbed his hat and threw it off the bridge onto the Mass Pike. Sly just grabbed him by the throat and started pounding on his head…"

"I've moved around a lot in my life. I've never really had a set home in all the years I've worked here at *Boston Baseball* and I can really find my bearings here at Fenway Park. I consider all these people like my family. And all these guys I've met… they've been my friends for the longest time, and that's about it."

Tim Dineen talked about working for me for eight or nine years and how before that he had been working on sausage carts around the ballpark since 1978. Chris recalled all the times he was handed tickets outside the park and got to go into the game for free.

Anthony, an authority on martial arts, sharp knives, and holistic medicine, called *Boston Baseball* "the best job I've ever had and also a form of therapy for me. I can convert my negative energy into useful positive energy. Every day is a funny story here.

"I don't like baseball. I think it sucks. There's nothing enjoyable about it. Deep down, I don't even like baseball fans. But I do like selling these magazines. That's about it."

Hai began by re-telling the longest-running *Boston Baseball* joke — "I just want to clarify that I didn't break the dolly" — and finished by doing an imitation of Sly doing a count out at the end of a big day, throwing down his money with exaggerated gestures and then running around pumping his fists in the air, swinging imaginary bats and hitting imaginary home runs.

"I remember my first day at *Boston Baseball*," Lemon told the camera. "We were working out of Mom & Pop's, and this bitch [pointing at me] wouldn't shake my hand.

"I think I speak for all my co-workers when I say that *Boston Baseball* is probably the best thing and the worst thing that happened to us. It's the best job you could ever have, because it's probably the most enjoyable and most entertaining job you could have.

"But I'd also say it's the worst job you could ever have, because after working here every other job is boring and lazy... I mean, what other job do you get to swear at the boss? There's no other job like this in the world. I like working here."

Watching the video later, I was struck by Lemon's awareness that *Boston Baseball* had been a mixed influence on him. As a teenager, it gave him a job, money and structure. *Boston Baseball* was a place where he excelled and was appreciated and listened to. Lemon thrived in that environment. He worked his butt off and he played a major role in our ballpark sales team.

As he got older, however, he needed more than a part-time seasonal job, and that's where *Boston Baseball* spoiled him. Lemon needed a real job and real money at the same time that he expected excitement, camaraderie, and independence. He wanted a job where he was trusted to do what needed to be done, where results were immediately rewarded, where he had the ear of his boss, where he could make an impact. And yet without a college degree, he had a terrible time finding one.

At one point he took the US Postal Service exam, scored well, was hired, and went to work driving a truck on a route in Roxbury. He'd regale us with tales of bureaucracy, stupidity, and outright corruption. The money was good, but the hours were long, and it wasn't for him. We had long conversations about what he should do with himself. Unlike me, Lemon was pretty good about asking for advice. But he wasn't very good about taking it.

September came; the strike didn't happen, but the street closure did. In my September column ("Lies the Red Sox Told Us") I did my best to expose the various untruths the Red Sox had told during their campaign for Yawkey Way:

Lie #1: Privatizing Yawkey Way was not about the money;

Lie #2: Privatizing Yawkey Way would allow the Red Sox to remain in Fenway Park;

Lie #3: Privatizing Yawkey Way would be a good thing for the fans; and

Lie #4: Privatizing Yawkey Way might not be such a bad thing for the vendors.

It was a brutal month. The team went into a tailspin and missed the postseason. The turnstiles went up, shutting us out of our most lucrative selling areas. It seemed as if my only recourse was through the courts.

I filed a suit in Federal court stating that by denying my hawkers access to a public street, my First Amendment rights were being violated. Named in the suit were the Red Sox, Aramark, the City of Boston, and the Boston Redevelopment Authority, whose classification of Yawkey Way as "blighted" had cleared the way for the City to lease the street to the Red Sox.

It was not at all clear that we would win our suit; what was clear was that we would be up against a formidable legal team. I still had hopes that one of the big non-profit foundations would take an interest in the case, but that still hadn't happened as the season ended and the lights went out at Fenway Park.

Not all was doom and gloom in 2002. My plans to build a replica of a historic vessel and sail it out of a North Shore port had finally come together.

Conceding that nobody in Beverly was ready to partner with me on a *Hannah* replica, I switched gears and began looking at Salem, where there was better access to the waterfront and many, many more tourists. Here, I felt that a modest vessel had a chance to operate at a small profit and be a valued addition to the community.

Harold Burnham, the Essex boatbuilder whom I had counted on to build the *Hannah*, suggested that I consider building a replica of the schooner *Fame*, a Salem privateer from the War of 1812. It was exactly the boat I was looking for — an easily-handled schooner, small enough to work in and out of Salem's shallow harbor, but big enough to pay for itself through public sails and charters. *Fame* was a Chebacco boat, a design that had originated right here in Essex, and the story of the original *Fame* was an exciting one, well-documented, with ties to people, places, and events all over the region.

In February of 2002 I had handed Harold a check so that he could begin drawing up plans and locating the wood for the project; in September, just days before the gates slammed shut on Yawkey Way, we held a keel-laying celebration at Harold's historic boatyard in Essex. We worked all winter long, building a new *Fame* in much the same way as the original had been built 200 years earlier.

It was a terrific project, one that I was hugely excited about. It certainly kept my mind off baseball all through that winter — except on those occasions when I was in court.

We had filed our suit, the Red Sox had been forced to respond to it, and we received some coverage in the media. However, none of the other vendors came forward to join me, and the legal foundations, while expressing interest, never did make a firm commitment. The Red Sox expressed no interest in reaching a compromise. I was on my own, facing a legal battle that my lawyer assured me could take years and would cer-

Anthony Tarallo

tainly cost me $100,000 in legal bills.

As much as I would have liked to pursue the case, I did not have the resources to fight the four heavyweight defendants, all of whom had legal teams at their beck and call. My attorney and I were forced to drop our case and accept my banishment from Yawkey Way.

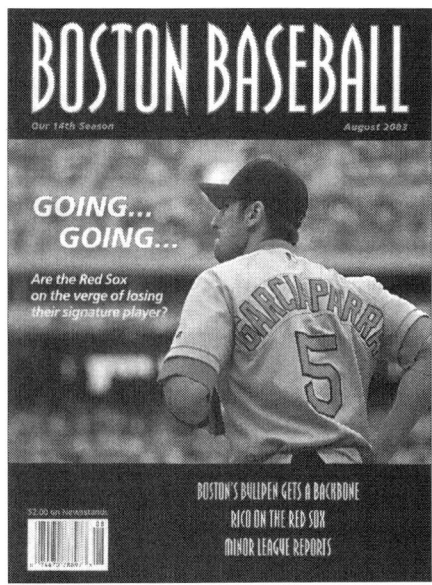

August, 2003

We returned to Fenway Park in April and took up the axe we had laid down in September. My Opening Day column declared that as far as the vendors outside the ballpark were concerned, it was the Red Sox, not the Yankees, who were the "Evil Empire."

Sure enough, sales were down. Sly was gone again, and I was often busy at the boatyard, but we had a solid crew of hawkers led by Ryan, Lemon, and John Freeman. We just didn't have the same access to the crowds that we used to have, especially with the Red Sox opening the gates earlier so as to take maximum advantage of their new concourse. It would take us most of the season to figure out how to get sales back to where they had been.

The Red Sox, after a disappointing end to the 2002 season, came on strong in 2003. David Ortiz emerged as a premier

Sly in the jungle

slugger, the centerpiece of an offense that would lead the AL in runs scored in 2003, 2004 and 2005. The pitching was good, but the Sox were still short a starter and a closer.

Boston finished second to New York for the sixth straight year despite winning 95 games, and the two teams met in a memorable ALCS that wasn't decided until the 11th inning of Game Seven, when Aaron Boone lofted a home run off Tim Wakefield.

Not all the pages of *Boston Baseball* were taken up with sniping at the front office. We ran a series of excerpts from Bill Lee's latest book that proved very popular with our readers, and in response to customer feedback, we began running head shots of all the Red Sox players in each issue.

On June 14, *Fame* was launched, and by July 25 she was carrying passengers out of Salem. Ads featuring the schooner and the summer day camp we run on board became a regular sight in the pages of *Boston Baseball*.

Late in the summer, I received a photo in the mail showing Sly, in full combat gear, deep in the jungle somewhere. In one hand he was holding an automatic rifle; in the other, the latest issue of *Boston Baseball*.

The photo appeared in our September issue, in honor of Sly and of all the American soldiers who were now serving overseas in places like Afghanistan, Iraq, and Southeast Asia.

The war on terror took on a different aspect at Fenway Park. Security had been tightened, with bags being searched and metal detectors installed at the turnstiles. Sadly, the team used "security reasons" to institute a number of pernicious regulations, such as banning fans from bringing drinks into the ballpark, then turning around and selling them bottled water for $4.25.

Not even the *Globe*, whose parent company owns 17% of the team, could let that pass. After a couple of pointed editorials and cartoons, the team modified their policy and allowed fans to bring in a single bottle of water.

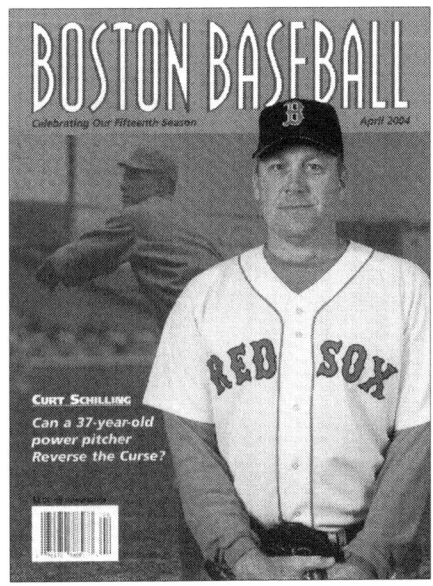

April, 2004

# 2004

Everybody knows what happened in 2004. But anyone who tells you they saw it coming is a liar.

True, the season began with a great deal of excitement. The team that had fallen one pitch short of reaching the World Series had gone out and signed a proven ace and big-game pitcher, Curt Schilling, and a lights-out closer, Keith Foulke.

From Boone's homer to Schilling's signing to the first day of spring training, everyone was talking about the Red Sox all winter long. The team sold 2.1 million tickets before the pitchers and catchers even reported to spring training. Could this, at long last, be the year?

The cover of our April issue featured Schilling in the foreground, Babe Ruth in the background, and asked "Can a 37-year-old power pitcher Reverse the Curse?"

Inside, we noted "A new sense of purpose and urgency… Everyone understands that the current nucleus of Pedro Martinez, Nomar Garciaparra, Manny Ramirez, Derek Lowe and Jason Varitek is about to be broken up. Will acquisitions such as Curt Schilling and Keith Foulke put this team over the top?"

Theoretically, the Sox now had a world-beating rotation of Schilling, Pedro Martinez, Derek Lowe, and Tim Wakefield. But by 2004 Pedro seemed to have lost something off his fastball; he was striking out fewer batters and walking more, giving up more hits and homers, and he posted his highest ERA to date, 3.90. Lowe, too, posted the highest ERA of his career, while Wakefield (12-10, 4.87) had a pedestrian season.

With Johnny Damon setting the table, the Red Sox featured the highest-scoring offense in baseball. Manny Ramirez led the league in homers and slugging, while he and David Ortiz finished 1-2 in extra-base hits and 2-3 in RBI. Still, despite all the runs, and pitching in front of a pretty good defense, Pedro won just 16 games, Lowe 14.

Right up until the end, there was little about the 2004 Red Sox that screamed "World Champions". The Sox lost three of their first five games, followed a terrific May with a lousy June, and went into the All-Star break at 48-38 — ten games over .500, but seven full games behind the Yankees. In fact, they were closer to third-place Tampa Bay than

July, 2004. The writing was on the wall for Nomar Garciaparra

they were to the front-running Bombers, and were tied with the low-budget Athletics for the wild-card berth.

At the trading deadline, a year's worth of rumors and innuendo were capped by the blockbuster trade of Nomar Garciaparra. Boston's long-time poster boy had missed half the team's games and was batting .321 with five homers when he was moved in a four-team deal with the Cubs, Twins, and Expos. In return, the Red Sox received Doug Mientkiewicz and Orlando Cabrera and saved about $3 million in payroll.

The cover of our August issue said it all: "Wild Card or Bust: which will it be for the underachieving 2004 Red Sox?"

That was the nadir. But then the Sox finally got hot. They won ten in a row from August 24 to September 3 and challenged the Yankees for first place before finishing three games out. It was the seventh straight year that Boston had finished second to New York.

They'd won 98 games, their highest total since 1978, but all that earned them was a trip to Anaheim. And if they survived, they'd likely have to face the Yankees again.

Well, there are plenty of great books you can read about the 2004 postseason. The ALCS alone provided enough material for a best-seller. Shortly after midnight on October 28, I called my father in Florida so we could watch together as Edgar Renteria bounced out to Keith

Foulke. The Red Sox were World Champions for the first time since 1918.

It is a truism in sports that the financial rewards of a winning season are only reaped once that season is over. But 2004 had been pretty good to us. Advertising sales were up, which was only to be expected given the unprecedented preseason buzz, and we managed to earn back half the sales we had lost in 2003 due to the closure of Yawkey Way. We did this by adding more hawkers, especially at either end of Yawkey Way, and experimenting with a variety of giveways along with the magazine.

We handed out tens of thousands of baseball cards, in packs of three or four, and for the first time printed up bumper stickers. Our 'Pokey for President' stickers, saluting slick-fielding Pokey Reese, were a big hit and turned up in all sorts of unexpected places.

In June we suffered a real loss. Doug Pappas, who had been writing for *Boston Baseball* since 1996, died while hiking at Big Bend National Park in Texas. He was just 42.

A nationally-recognized authority on the business of baseball, with over fifty published articles on the subject, Doug was the legal counsel for SABR, the Society for American Baseball Research. His concise and informative 'Baseball Biz' column, and his two season-long features, the first on John Harrington's rise to power, and the second examining the track record of publicly-funded ballparks around baseball, represented the best of *Boston Baseball*.

Searching for a way to honor Doug's memory, I decided we would provide free advertising for the environmental and human rights groups that Doug had cared about. We ran full-page ads for the Sierra Club, Greenpeace, Stop Global Warming and Amnesty International for the remainder of the 2004 season.

Closer to home, we also lost a hawker during the season, the first time that had happened.

"Jimbo" was in his second year of hawking magazines for us. He died while the Red Sox were on the road. He was a recovered alcoholic, I

141

August, 2004

believe — a sweet man, a simple guy, delighted to help out and genuinely living one day at a time.

   With Doug Pappas gone, Glenn Stout became our cleanup hitter, the guy we counted on for big hits. In our September issue, Glenn went beyond the 'Curse of the Bambino' fairy tale to the roots of the story, and what he found there was lies and prejudice.

   Many Red Sox fans think they know the decades-old story of Harry Frazee and the sale of Babe Ruth. But that version was concocted in October, 1986 by New York *Times* writer George Vecsey, who had to rewrite his column in a hurry after the ball rolled through Bill Buckner's legs. It was later embroidered in a book by Dan Shaughnessy called *The Curse of the Bambino.*

   The problem with the whole 'Curse' story was that it was largely based on the writings of the late Fred Lieb, a legendary sportswriter who was also an unprincipled bigot. Lieb was perfectly willing to fabricate stories in order to reinforce his own twisted perceptions.

   Lieb pounced on the mistaken impression that Frazee was a Jew and rewrote Red Sox history with Frazee as the villain. His book, *The Boston Red Sox*, became the standard history of the team, and his fabrication went unquestioned for decades, until refuted by Glenn and Dick

Johnson in *Red Sox Century*, published in 2000.

One reason we were able to win back some of the sales we'd lost on Yawkey Way was Sly's return from active service. Sly immediately jumped into a heated competition with John Freeman for the top spot. Sly won four of our six homestands that year, while John won one and Lemon captured the other.

For the postseason, we published one magazine for the ALDS and ALCS and another for the World Series, which was partly new material and partly picked-up material from the ALDS/ALCS issue. We didn't have much experience with the playoffs at that point, and our postseason publications weren't as complete as they would be in later years. Still, they sold like hotcakes.

From a publishing perspective, the postseason is tough. Sure, it represents extra games and more opportunities to make money. However, it also involves publishing an extra issue, and printing up enough copies for the ALDS and ALCS without any assurance that the Sox will actually advance. If there aren't a lot of postseason home games, or if the team gets knocked out early, I lose.

The best case, with a team that has home-field advantage in all three series, is 11 home games. Worst case is a road team that gets swept in the first round. One home game — *adios*.

In 2004 we had six games, a result of the Sox being the road team in the ALDS and ALCS and of their sweeping both the Angels and Cardinals. Sweeps aren't good for business.

At least in 2004 and 2007 we had the opportunity to move our remaining magazines during the victory parades. We stayed home in 2004 because of the rain, but we did well in 2007, selling outside Fenway Park and all along the parade route to City Hall.

I spent the entire afternoon hopping in and out of my station wagon, selling magazines, delivering magazines, double-parking, navigating around the street closures. It was a long, long day — but worth the effort.

Too bad the weather wasn't better for the parade in 2004. It will never again be like it was in '04, when Red Sox fans were blowing off 86 years worth of steam. I remember watching the parade on TV, with the Red Sox players riding the Duck Boats in the rain, thinking *Damn, I could have made a lot of money today.*

The parade was just the beginning of the post-championship hoopla. The *Globe*, the *Herald*, *Sports Illustrated*, *The Sporting News*, and everyone else you could name commemorated the event with special issues. And then the hardcover books started coming out!

Unlike all of those publications. *Boston Baseball* relies on event sales to be profitable. No event, no profits. I'm sure our subscribers would have loved a commemorative issue, and I am sure we would have sold some on the newsstands, but not enough to give us a return on our investment. We decided to save our ammo for April 2005, when the Red Sox would be raising their banner at Fenway Park as the Yankees watched from the visiting dugout.

In the meantime, the magazines, books, and DVDs kept coming. The hawkers kept me posted as to which of them appeared in which DVD. Cameramen have always loved to film my hawkers outside the ballpark when they're trying to capture the fun and excitement of coming to Fenway.

On Opening Day, or for a big game, local and national film crews are always prowling the streets looking for some local color, and my guys are it. They get a huge kick out of being on the evening news, on the promo for an upcoming game on ESPN or Fox, or on a DVD that people will be watching for decades to come. Lemon was even incorporated into a baseball video game.

The rumor around the ballpark was that when the Red Sox' official DVD came out, Mayor Menino complained because he wasn't included. I can't really blame him, considering all he's done for the team — renting them Yawkey Way, for example! The DVD was re-edited to include Menino, and everyone was happy.

# 2005

I said earlier that the financial rewards of a winning season are only reaped once that season is over. This was certainly true in 2005. Magazine sales were up once again, although not quite where they had been before the closure of Yawkey Way. But ad sales were through the roof, as the dramatic 2004 postseason and the ensuing celebrations reminded everyone how important the Red Sox are to New England. When they're winning, all eyes are on them, and everyone wants to be associated with a winner.

We had so many ad pages sold that our April 2005 magazine ran to 108 pages, our biggest ever, and we kicked off the season with a huge Opening Day as fans snapped up souvenirs of the banner-raising.

On the field, nothing could live up to '04. Although the Red Sox won 95 games, they finished second to the Yankees for the eighth straight year. The team had decided to let Pedro Martinez walk away, and although the offense was still strong they didn't have quite enough pitching to repeat. The club made the playoffs, but were swept by the Chicago White Sox, who were en route to their own long-awaited World Championship.

This was the worst-case postseason scenario — one home game, goodbye. So as well as we did during the season, we did end on a down note with a money-losing postseason issue.

Still, how could we complain? Overall, revenues were up for the ninth straight year. We added more great features to the magazine. Former GM Lou Gorman had written a book about his career, and having been such a jerk to the poor guy while he was running the Red Sox, it was only right that we publish excerpts from it and let Lou tell his side of the story with his usual good humor and humility.

In 2005 for the first time we began publishing profiles of the current Red Sox, a feature I had admired in other baseball publications such as *The Grand Salami* but had not adopted for *Boston Baseball*.

*The Grand Salami* was Seattle's version of *Boston Baseball*. It had started up a few years after *Baseball Underground* in Boston and *GameDay* in Baltimore. Although not quite so comprehensive as either of those publications, *The Grand Salami* sold for $2 almost from the beginning, and they made an early move to thick, glossy paper stock. It's a nice magazine to look at.

Jon Wells is the publisher of *The Grand Salami*, and like the guys in Baltimore, he's had a much easier time dealing with the home team than I have. But there are other publishers who've run afoul of the home team, or the local authorities.

When the Colorado Rockies were playing their inaugural season at Mile High Stadium and setting all those attendance records, two local entrepreneurs started up their own alternative baseball programs, one called *The Game Program* and the other *The Homestand Flyer*.

When the team moved into brand-new Coors Field, they tried to ban the alternative programs from selling on the walkways around the park, and it ended up in court. The ACLU agreed to take the case, and the District Court found in favor of the publishers. The Rockies appealed the case to the Colorado Supreme Court, where the judgment was affirmed.

There was a publication called *The Blue Line* that was started up by a couple of Chicago Blackhawks fans and sold outside Chicago Stadium and later the United Center during the 1990s. *The Blue Line* was more along the lines of the English soccer 'zines, some of which are pretty outrageous. The Blackhawks management hated *The Blue Line*, which satirized club owner Bill Wirtz. They also didn't care for publisher Mark Weinberg, who twice used his law degree to sue the team.

In 1995 he sued the team for refusing media credentials to his publication. In 1997 he represented a group of independent peanut vendors who were protesting a decision by the Blackhawks not to allow outside snacks inside the arena. He lost both suits.

Twice Weinstein was arrested for "obstructing pedestrian traffic" while selling his publication, and a third time while selling copies of a book he had written about Wirtz' ownership of the Blackhawks. Weinstein took the City to court, claiming false arrest, and won a settlement.

Another publisher, Jay Roper, liked what he saw in publications such as *Baseball Underground*, *GameDay*, and *The Grand Salami* and decided he would produce a similar magazine with editions in different cities, including Chicago, Cleveland, and Atlanta. He recruited some of my hawkers to help him. Sly and Tim Michaud went to Atlanta to work on that edition, and they still enjoy retelling their adventures giving away free popsicles with each magazine during the sultry Georgia summers.

Sly and Ryan went on a road trip to see Wrigley Field a few years later and looked up Roper, offering to help him sell his Chicago magazine for the day. They claim they were sent to marginal gates, but still blew away all of Roper's salespeople. A recent online search didn't turn up any of Roper's publications, so I believe they are all defunct.

Franchising the *Baseball Underground* concept was something I gave a lot of thought to during the first few years, especially after we got all that publicity in 1992 and baseball fans began calling me up from all over the country, asking how they could start a similar magazine in their town.

Of course, there were many markets in which the idea just wasn't going to work. Where stadiums were located on land owned or leased by the team, independent vendors were simply not allowed. Rodney Paul once sent me a photo of a sign at Oakland-Alameda Coliseum which declares NO SELLING OF ANYTHING.

In other towns, the fan base wasn't big enough, or intense enough, to support an independent magazine.

But by 1993 I had decided that I wanted to get married and raise a family; I didn't want to spend seven months a year shuttling from one baseball city to another, publishing multiple magazines and managing multiple sales forces and ad sales teams. Instead, I would try to expand my business within the New England market, which was the thinking behind my Boston College publication as well as my Cape Cod League program, my partnership with the Lowell Spinners, and my repeated efforts to find common ground with the Red Sox.

Every year I developed a different business plan. One year it was a magazine devoted to Ivy League sports, which I thought would be an attractive niche publication for upscale advertisers; then it was a glossy sports monthly called *New England Pro*, focusing on New England's professional sports franchises. Another year it was a free daily sports newspaper — essentially a sports edition of the *Metro*, several years before the *Metro* appeared.

Most of these ideas never made it past the business-plan stage; others were bandied about with potential partners and investors, and constantly I was being distracted by other ventures, such as the Rivals.com network and the Red Sox, Celtics, Bruins, and BC sites they engaged me to run. And then, in 2002, I decided to go in a completely different direction and build a schooner.

Do I regret not starting a chain of baseball magazines across the country? Not for a minute.

In May of 2005, Manny Ramirez hit his 400th career home run. We had continued giving out baseball cards and bumper stickers occasionally when we thought sales needed a boost, and now we printed up 5,000 postcards commemorating Manny's big hit and handed them out free with the magazine. That worked well, and we produced similar cards when Curt Schilling won his 200th game and in 2008 when Manny hit his 500th home run.

The hawkers love giveaways, because it gives them another selling point, something else to yell about, and of course the giveaways don't cost them anything! So they're constantly coming up with new giveaway ideas, which is great.

Of course, they aren't always very realistic about what we can afford to give away. This leads to suggestions that we give away everything from Red Sox key chains to pennants, posters, beads and glow-sticks. In 2005 I was laughing most of these suggestions off. A year later I'd be paying much closer attention.

A free postcard
handed out in May, 2005

# 2006

By 2006 the Red Sox had returned to earth. Johnny Damon was a Yankee, Pedro Martinez was a Met, Derek Lowe and Nomar Garciaparra were Dodgers. Jason Varitek hit .238. Keith Foulke, who had saved 32 games for the World Championship club, saved zero games in 2006.

David Ortiz (54 HR) had a huge year, and the offense was decent, but the pitching struggled. Josh Beckett, the new ace, won 16 games but posted an ERA of 5.01 and surrendered 36 home runs in his AL debut. Despite their $120 million payroll, the Sox were an average ballclub. For the first time since 1997 they failed to win or place, falling to third behind the Toronto Blue Jays.

Still, the season wasn't a total waste, witnessing as it did the break-though of two pitching prospects who would figure prominently a year later — starter Jon Lester and closer Jonathan Papelbon.

And we did find things to write about. We ran a series of excerpts from Tim Gay's excellent book about Tris Speaker, one of the Red Sox' early stars. We partnered with former Red Sox medical director Dr. Bill Morgan on an injury report column. We ran an expose, complete with stakeout photos, on the autographed-items trade that had become such big business on websites like eBay.

When Johnny Damon came to town as a Yankee for the first time we printed up a WANTED poster similar to the one we had printed for Roger Clemens.

"Warning!" read the poster, which depicted a clean-shaven Damon in pinstripes. "He has recently changed his appearance!"

With the team struggling for the first time in several years, sales would have been down in any event. But in 2006 we had to confront a serious challenge.

Just as there had been nothing to stop me from launching my own magazine and selling it outside Fenway Park, there was nothing to stop anyone else from doing the same thing. Over the years we had faced several different competitors, people who saw the success of *Boston Baseball* and tried to grab a share of our business. None of them had lasted very long.

April, 2006

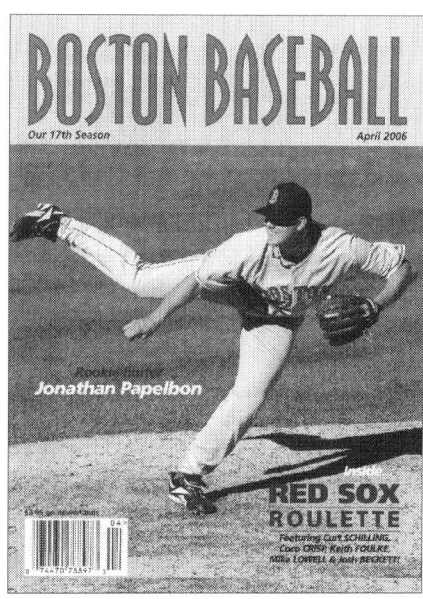

Still, I was always conscious of the potential for people to come into our market and compete with us. After 2002, when we began to attract national advertisers, I knew it was only a matter of time before some of the local media players started to take a closer look at our market.

During the 2006 season, the free *Metro* newspaper announced that they were launching a ballpark publication called *GameDay*. Like the *Metro*, it would be a 12-page short-tab newspaper printed in color. Like the *Metro*, it would be free.

As competition goes, this was alarming. It was more alarming, in fact, than when the Red Sox had slashed the price of their official book in half. After all, 'FREE' is hard to beat.

Furthermore, the *Metro* had the blessing of the Red Sox, who stuffed copies inside their own official program and declared *GameDay* to be the "official gameday publication of the Boston Red Sox." The *Globe*, whose parent company owns 17% of the Red Sox, was also a large shareholder in the *Metro*.

Still, *GameDay* was just 12 pages on newsprint, and naturally it lacked the depth of our 88-page magazine. While many people buy *Boston Baseball* as a souvenir, or something to get autographed, the flimsy *GameDay* did not qualify on that score. They had rosters, box scores, and standings, but no stats. The scorecard was decent, but not as good as ours.

Our work was cut out for us. We were going to lose sales to *GameDay*. The question was, how many? We had to continue to put our very best foot forward on the streets around the ballpark and make sure people were aware of our selling points.

We also decided to get more aggressive with our giveaways. Between us, Sly and I acquired over 50,000 baseball cards, many of them vintage cards from the 1970s and 1980s, and we sorted them into packs of three and four cards apiece to hand out, mostly to kids. We made sure people knew that we were giving out free pencils with every purchase. We also stepped up our production of bumper stickers. A popular sticker from 2006 was "You Can't Touch / BIG PAPI in the Clutch". We went through two printings of 10,000 apiece.

All the giveaways cut into my margin, of course, but they kept the hawkers upbeat and motivated. That was crucial, because from the very beginning there was friction between my hawkers and the crew that were handing out *GameDay*.

First of all, *GameDay* had set up a series of portable newspaper boxes around the ballpark, which upset us because it was exactly the sort of thing that Code Enforcement had been telling me I couldn't do for the previous 16 years. Were there different rules for the *Globe* and the *Metro* than there were for small businesses?

I walked around the ballpark, taking photos of the *GameDay* stands, and of the trash cans and gutters stuffed with discarded copies. Eventually, Code Enforcement started to challenge and even fine the *GameDay* staff over their stands and the mess they were creating on the streets.

Secondly, *GameDay* was clearly aimed at putting *Boston Baseball* out of business, and as such they placed their workers right next to mine, sometimes two guys for each one of mine. It made sense, of course, but it was a highly confrontational strategy.

All the vendors around the ballpark have to respect each other's space, or the tone soon gets nasty. Remember, everyone you see is working on commission. They need to move product. One of the first things I tell my new hawkers is to respect the other vendors and to give them room. We can move around; most of them can't, so it's up to us not to crowd them or to stand in front of them, but to keep moving.

In the few areas where our hawkers have to stand close to other vendors, they yell in turns. We've all learned to get along. If you're ever at the park and see two vendors trying to out-shout one another, something is going on. There's a new kid on the block.

Well, it's bad enough if two hawkers are side by side and one is selling sausages and the other is selling t-shirts. If they're actually competing with each other, then you've got trouble. With hawkers yelling over each other for two and half hours at a stretch, you can imagine that with a crew of young, spirited people, tempers flared.

We could not afford to back down, and I let my hawkers know it. To their credit, they rose to the occasion. They competed hard, they kept their noses clean, and the magazines got sold. Late in the season, we sold our two millionth copy of *Boston Baseball*.

At the end of the season, however, the numbers were not pretty. Some of that was due to the disappointing performance of the Red Sox, but *GameDay* certainly contributed. I spent the winter taking long walks around my neighborhood in Boxford, where we had moved in 2004, turning over different strategies for defeating *GameDay*.

Advertising sales worried me. Print ad sales were slipping everywhere as people put more of their marketing budgets into their websites, and into online marketing. USP, which had bought out PSP, was so big

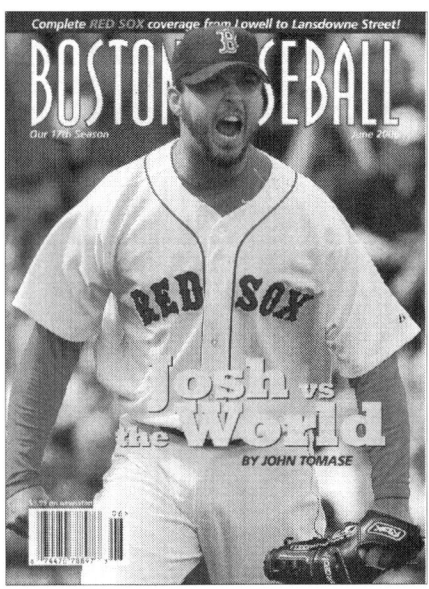

June, 2006

and I was such a tiny part of their overall business that they rarely bothered to communicate with me. All I knew was that ad sales were down.

I was convinced that we could be selling more ads to local and regional businesses. Should I invest in a full-time advertising salesperson? Were two or three part-timers better than one full-time person?

Ballpark sales worried me. Sly and the other hawkers were pushing for a giveaway every single game of the season. Although I worried that the hawkers would become dependent on giveaways, instead of focusing on the selling points of the magazine, I thought it might prove necessary.

Pricing worried me. During the ten years we had sold the magazine for $1, there was no question in my mind that *Boston Baseball* was an outrageous value. I had thought the same was true at $2, until the free *GameDay* showed up. Would we regain sales if we went back to $1? Was price an issue at all? If not, maybe we should increase the price! The Red Sox' official scorecard/magazine book was now $5, so even at $3, we were a bargain.

I considered putting together a new proposal for the Red Sox. My first proposal had met with no response, and soon thereafter we had tangled over Yawkey Way, so we had never really sat down to discuss working together. Was this the time, or would they take any overture from me to be a sign of weakness?

I pondered major changes in my business model. What if I repositioned *Boston Baseball* as a free publication? Would advertising generate enough revenue to keep the glossy, full-color magazine format? What would happen to our newsstand and subscription sales if the magazine were available for free at the ballpark?

Most of all, I wondered what sort of reception *GameDay* was meeting with from advertisers. They'd had surprisingly little advertising in 2006, and I was sure they were operating at a frightful loss. The key to their business plan was to convince advertisers that they were going to be a major player at the ballpark. Advertisers would allow *GameDay* to expand beyond its current 12 pages to a bigger and more complete format that would be a more formidable competitor for *Boston Baseball*.

I didn't think *GameDay* was going to be an easy sell. With free publications, it's hard to tell how many copies are actually being read, and how many are going undistributed or being thrown away unread. Copies of *GameDay* filled the trash cans and littered the streets around Fenway Park, and I had the photos to prove it. Companies do not like to see their advertising buys in the trash.

However, *GameDay* would have all the ad-sales resources of the *Metro* and, for all I knew, the *Globe* at its disposal. This was a tremendous advantage, one that worried me greatly as I paced my neighborhood.

In the end I adopted several strategies for dealing with *GameDay*. I accepted that in the short term, we were going to have to be aggressive with giveaways, and made plans to acquire more baseball cards and bumper stickers. I stepped up my efforts to sell advertising directly rather than relying on USP.

I decided to make a commitment to using a professional designer. For many years, since Marie Haines had redesigned the magazine and then moved on, I'd been laying out the magazine myself. The price was right, and I was competent and consistent if not especially talented. Competent and consistent was no longer good enough, however. We needed to have eye-catching covers.

I hired Donni Richman, who had been laying out *Patriots Weekly*, and I agreed to get him better photos to work with, even if that meant buying them from the AP and Getty.

And I did send a proposal to the Red Sox, who agreed to a meeting. We met in one of the Fenway Park conference rooms overlooking Yawkey Way, right above where the Will Call window used to be.

Waiting for the meeting to start, I looked down onto the street where I had spent the last 19 summers of my life. I wondered how many times Red Sox executives had stood at these windows, looking down at me and my hawkers.

The meeting was not productive. The Red Sox thought I was dealing from weakness, that *GameDay* had brought me to my knees. Larry Lucchino asked me twice, rather pointedly, why I had chosen this particular time to request a meeting.

They did not seem especially interested in my proposal for working together to publish the mother of all Red Sox magazines, but we did have a general discussion about the various obstacles we'd have to overcome in order to work together. I enjoyed the opportunity to meet face to face with Dr. Charles Steinberg, the former VP for Public Affairs, and team COO Mike Dee.

Dee struck me as an extremely smart man with an open mind. Steinberg worried me. He saw the official magazine primarily as a public relations tool. My vision for our joint publication was for a magazine

September, 2006

that emphasized news and reporting rather than PR. I wanted regular Q&As with Theo Epstein, Ben Cherrington, and Mike Hazen, not puff pieces on the Red Sox Foundation. I wanted head shots of the team's June draftees, not photos of the Red Sox players' wives painting a community center.

I got the sense that if I were to work with the Red Sox, my liaison would be Dr. Steinberg, and I don't think we would have been on the same page.

That said, it wasn't a surprise or a disappointment when the meeting went nowhere, and I returned to planning for the 2007 season. With the ballyhooed signing of Japanese League ace Daisuke Matsuzaka, I thought there was an opportunity for us to run some unique promotions and get off to a good start.

Lemon was in Taiwan, teaching English, and volunteered his services as our man in the Far East. He had previously worked with suppliers in Taiwan and Thailand on various little projects, such as printing up t-shirts for the hawkers.

He arranged to have 10,000 headbands and 20,000 Japanese-style "beaters" made up in red and white, with "*Boston Baseball* Welcomes Daisuke Matsuzaka" in both English and Japanese along with the rising-sun flag. Beaters were a Japanese baseball tradition, long tubes that, when inflated, could be beaten together to make a serious racket.

They looked terrific, nobody else had them, and even with the cost of shipping to the United States (Hai drove to New Jersey in a rented van to pick them up at the dock) the price wasn't much more than what we were paying for postcards and bumper stickers.

If only Matsuzaka could stay healthy and get off to a good start, we were going to *own* April at the ballpark.

April 2007

# 2007

Daisuke Matsuzaka did his part. He made his first major league start on April 5 in Kansas City. He walked one, recorded 10 strikeouts, and retired 10 consecutive batters in a 4-1 win.

He was, however, beaten 3-0 by Félix Hernández (who pitched a one hitter) and the Seattle Mariners in his Fenway Park debut. We debuted new *Boston Baseball* shirts that day, with Japanese flags on the sleeve.

Matsuzaka was defeated again, 2-1, by the Toronto Blue Jays in his third start despite striking out 10. He was the first pitcher to strike out 10 or more batters in two of his first three big-league starts since Fernando Valenzuela in 1981.

Red Sox fans were gaga over Matsuzaka, and the headbands were a huge hit. Initially, however, people didn't know what to make of the beaters. The hawkers had to blow up a pair and display them so that people knew what they were talking about. Whenever Matsuzaka made a start at Fenway, I'd give the hawkers the choice of headbands or beaters, and they opted for headbands until the headbands were all gone.

At that point we switched to the beaters, only to have the Code Enforcement Police jump in and tell us it was illegal to hand them out. Apparently, at the Boston Marathon in April, similar noisemakers had been banned, and that ban was going to be extended to our beaters. This was bad news, as I had 10,000 of them in my garage at home. Despite giving them out baseball card shows and other events over the past two years, many of them are still there.

Didn't matter. We had plenty of other things to hand out. Sly had brokered a deal with SupahFans which gave us 10,000 bumper stickers each month to hand out in exchange for a free ad in the magazine. Between the headbands, the beaters, the bumper stickers, and baseball cards, we had a giveaway every day, and our hawkers used them to great effect.

By the all-star break, the *GameDay* crew — who'd been overheard boasting that they were going to put us out of business — was visibly dispirited.

And you know what they say: a rising tide lifts all boats. In this case, the tide was the 96-win regular season. On April 18 the Red Sox took over first place with an 8-5 record and never relinquished it. The Red Sox finished first for the first time since 1995, which was also the last time they had finished ahead of the Yankees.

Boston's pitching was superb. Josh Beckett turned in exactly the season the Red Sox had acquired him to have, going 20-7 with a 3.27 ERA. Forty-year-old Tim Wakefield tied his career high with 17 wins, while Matsuzaka won 15. In the bullpen, Hideki Okajima proved to be nearly as valuable as his compatriot, posting a 2.22 ERA over 66 games, and Jonathan Papelbon was, once again, lights out.

The offense was powerful and well-balanced. David Ortiz and Manny Ramirez remained the big guns, but they were supported by strong years from Jason Varitek, Kevin Youkilis, Rookie of the Year Dustin Pedroia, and Mike Lowell.

Newcomer J. D. Drew was a disappointment, especially given his fat contract. There was speculation that his signing was connected to the Matsuzaka deal, as Scott Boras represented both players. When his production failed to match his $14 million salary, fans began referring to him as 'Nancy' Drew.

But 23-year-old Jacoby Ellsbury woke everyone up with an electrifying debut, batting .353 in 33 games and picking up nine postseason hits.


This was the 40th anniversary of the Red Sox Impossible Dream season, a watershed — probably *the* watershed — in the history of the Boston franchise. To commemorate this event we published a series of excerpts from Rico Petrocelli's book, *Tales from the Impossible Dream*. Much has been written about that team and that season, but Rico's view from the inside made it the best of the many anniversary books that were published that year.

Rico has been a contributor to *Boston Baseball* for many years, going back to his years as a coach and instructor in the Red Sox farm system. At different times he has contributed to our minor league and major league coverage as well as writing a series of instructional articles aimed at coaches and players. He's always a delight to work with.

We also published a guest column in the April issue by former WWF wrestler The Ultimate Warrior.

Steroids were in the news just then, and it so happened that Lemon, a wrestling fan from childhood, was in touch with him. It wasn't the most coherent column we've ever published, but it did provide valuable insight into the mindset of those who take performance-enhancing drugs, as The Ultimate Warrior has courageously admitted he did.

Twice in 2007, we printed two different covers for the same issue. In June, when the Giants visited Fenway, we sold magazines with a special Barry Bonds cover. Bonds was facing steroid allegations at the same time he was nearing Hank Aaron's career homer-run mark, and we quickly sold out the special covers. In July we did it again, printing an alternate cover featuring red-hot rookie Dustin Pedroia.

At the time, I thought alternate covers were a terrific way to boost circulation and also feature some players who otherwise might not appear on a cover. Remember, we only have six to eight covers each year. Back in the 1990s, when the team was bad, it was hard to identify six players that we wanted to put on the cover. We'd go with two Roger Clemens covers and two Mo Vaughn covers, and then the remaining covers might be Scott Fletcher, Jeff Russell, Darren Bragg, Scott Cooper, and so on.

In recent years the reverse has been true — the Sox have more players deserving of cover treatment than we have issues. It's a good problem to have.

I was surprised, then, to find that some fans were confused and upset by the alternative covers. Although the magazines were clearly marked as "June" or "July", fans assumed that a different cover meant a completely different magazine. When they got to their seats, opened the magazine, and found it was the same issue they had purchased earlier in the month, they were mad.

We also had some problems with subscribers. People who collect the magazines were upset that they were mailed only one of the two covers. Others were content to receive one copy, but they usually wanted the cover that they didn't get!

I asked readers for feedback on the covers in my August column and got a mixed response. As a result, we've tabled the alternate covers for the time being, but I'd like to get to back to them if we can figure out way to make sure people understand what we're doing.

Speaking of Bonds, I was on the field for one of those games. For the first time in over a decade, the Red Sox agreed to give me one pre-game field credential a month. It was fun being on the field again, and

# IT AIN'T OVER TIL THE BIG PAPI SWINGS!

we did use quite a few of the photos I took.

But I was struck by the change in the atmosphere from twenty years ago to today. I can remember spring training games with just five or six media on the field. Nowadays even a regular-season game is a major event, with media everywhere and a packed gallery of VIPs and hangers-on roped off behind the batting cage.

One thing you do get to see on the field before games is the fraternization between the Red Sox and the visiting players. It gives you a good sense of who is liked and respected. Barry Bonds, when he came to Fenway, was too hot to touch; several Red Sox greeted him but did not linger. Bonds was so much the center of attention that hardly anyone noticed Willie Mays, who was traveling with the Giants, but he and David Ortiz had a quiet chat behind the cage.

Alternate covers were not our only circulation initiative; ever since 2006 we have been binding Business Reply Cards into the magazine. These are the postage-paid cards, blown in or bound in to the magazine, which encourage people to sign up for a subscription. This seems obvious, doesn't it? Every magazine uses them. But I had made a conscious decision years ago not to pursue the subscription market.

I felt that subscriptions were a declining market, and that the folks who couldn't get to a game to buy the magazine would increasingly go online to get their Red Sox fix rather than sign up to receive something via the temperamental US Mail. The mail market, I felt, was made up of older fans and it was a market that would continue to shrink as they aged.

Well, it has, but with the recent success of the team and the growth of the magazine I've found there's still a strong demand for subscriptions. Rather then fight it, I decided to encourage it, and took the long-delayed step of binding cards into the magazine. They've been an unqualified success.

And then there were the bumper stickers. Above and beyond the 10,000 stickers a month we got from SupahFans, we printed up our own.

"IT AINT OVER 'TIL THE BIG PAPI SWINGS" was a popular sticker in red, white, and blue, while the simple "YOOOOOUK!" in green and white has gone through two printings.

As the pennant race heated up in 2007, the Red Sox acquired Eric Gagne, formerly a top closer for the Dodgers, to shore up their bullpen. Gagne was a disaster. He was so bad that it would have been funny — if the Yankees hadn't been breathing down our necks.

I designed a pinstriped sticker that read "GAGNE IS A YANKEE SPY". Nobody liked the idea, least of all my father, but it tickled my funny bone, so I printed them up. It was the only negative sticker we had done, and reaction was mixed. We distributed most of them and had a small pile left over, which we gave away the next year when he came back to town with the Brewers. He was pitching terribly for them, too.

In my September column, I returned to one of my favorite topics — the occasional disdain shown by the Red Sox toward their fans.

This had been a major problem with the previous ownership, who took their fans and their season-ticketholders for granted. The new ownership, I felt, was far better in this regard — until they came up with the idea of charging people to call themselves fans.

I'd toyed with the idea of a fan club years earlier. I had assumed that to entice people to join, they would have to receive some benefits with real value. The Red Sox, in a move that was either brilliant or shameless, dispensed with the benefits and somehow persuaded thousands of fans that they needed to send the team money in order to be included in 'Red

# YOOOOOUK!

Sox Nation.'

Near as I can tell, this term was popularized by *Globe* columnist Dan Shaughnessy as a description (at various times admiring and contemptuous) of the passionate but unstable masses who follow the Olde Towne Team. The Red Sox embraced it, sensing yet another way to cash in.

Fans were urged to prove their loyalty by signing up for a membership in Red Sox Nation, paying anywhere for $14.95 to $199 for such exclusive benefits as a membership card and a 10% discount at the grossly overpriced Red Sox Team Store. Another benefit was the right to enter at Gate C, which had formerly been reserved for college students, drunks, and fans with inflatable dolls.

Baseball teams in less frenzied markets would be embarrassed to publish such an offer.

My October column continued to take the Sox to task. When the team is doing well, people don't ask questions. But I wanted to point out that the Red Sox were joined in baseball's Final Four by three teams — the Indians, Diamondbacks, and Rockies — who had roughly one-third of Boston's payroll, and whose tickets and concessions were far more reasonable.

Is it really necessary, I asked, for everything Red Sox to be as expensive as it is? How do we justify rooting for a team that spent three times as much money in order to win the same number of games? Especially when it's our money they're spending!

It wasn't John Henry who gave that $51 million posting fee to the Seibu Lions, or paid J. D. Drew $14 million to hit eleven home runs. No, that was you and me! That was our money, the money we spent on tickets, on NESN, on food and drinks and souvenirs.

The Red Sox routinely lead all of baseball in the Fan Consumer Index, a measure of how expensive it is to attend baseball games for a family of four. When the Red Sox spend three times as much as other teams, they have to charge three times as much.

Like I said, when the team is losing, people are quick to bitch about how expensive everything is, but when they're winning? Don't ask, don't tell.

Red Sox Nation? How about 'Sucker Nation'?

The postseason was good to us. The Sox swept the Angels in the ALDS, went the distance in defeating Cleveland in the ALCS, and once again swept the World Series, this time stunning the red-hot Colorado Rockies.

This time we finally got our postseason issue right. We went with more pages and heavier stock and charged $5. The magazine looked great and sold well. We had to go head to head with a crew of guys from Philadelphia who'd been sent up to sell Major League Baseball's official ALCS and World Series programs, but that posed no difficulties. They put two or three hawkers on each of the busiest spots, but we still kicked their butts. My hawkers enjoyed showing them how we do it in Boston.

Once the postseason games were factored in, our ballpark sales were up nearly 25%. We'd gained back all the sales we'd lost to Yawkey Way and to *GameDay*. The only way to explain it was that as the novelty of *GameDay* wore off, the fans had returned to *Boston Baseball*.

Furthermore, *GameDay* had failed to boost their advertising revenues, which meant they were continuing to hemorrhage money. Operating at a loss meant that they weren't able to grow the publication as we had in our early years, plowing the profits back into the business so that every issue was bigger and better. By midsummer there were media reports that the *Metro* was ready to pull the plug on *GameDay*, which they did at the end of the season.

Overcoming the challenge that *GameDay* presented was a real accomplishment, especially as they had every possible advantage. They had all the resources of the Red Sox, the *Globe*, and the *Metro* at their disposal — printing presses, a newsroom full of professional journalists and photographers, a full-time advertising sales force, and unlimited access to the Red Sox staff and players.

Our one advantage was that we had been working our butts off for almost twenty years to give the fans the publication they wanted. As fans ourselves, we had a pretty good idea of what that was.

At the time, it was no big deal. We simply showed up every day and worked hard to make the best magazine we could and to sell as many of them as possible. But once it was over, looking back, the hawkers who were with me in 2006 and 2007 shared a sense of achievement.

Guys who had been with me for many years, like Sly, Ryan, Lemon, and Hai, could remember what it was like going head to head with the Red Sox in the 1990s. They knew what it felt like to be out there selling magazines and feel like the future of the business was in their hands.

We had to sell as many as we could, we had to sell more than the Red Sox did, we couldn't let them beat us, because it was wrong that they should win just because they were bigger and better-connected than we were.

Now the newer hawkers, like Joe Morelli and John Freeman and Steph and Mike and Chooch knew what that felt like.

We felt that while they were the official magazine, we were the *real* magazine — a magazine that had grown and thrived because it was in touch with the fans. *Give the people what they want* had been our motto, not *Tell 'em what we want them to hear.*

That's not to say all was sweetness and light in those years. We had our usual share of drama at the ballpark.

The fighting wasn't over who would be the top seller every month. Sly won every homestand in 2006, 2007 and 2008. He had the ballpark crowds eating out of his hands. Fans gave him tips, they brought him home-baked cookies, they wanted to have their picture taken with him. It seemed like he was on a first-name basis with everyone inside and outside of the park.

Sly had also been working hard to launch his own sports memorabilia business, buying and selling at shows and on the internet and eventually launching his own website, Beantown-collectibles.com.

He acquired a license to distribute MLB, NFL, and NBA merchandise, and produced his own line of commemorative pins. In 2007 he obtained a permit to operate souvenir carts on the street after the game, and with his characteristic determination and energy he put together small, mobile carts that could be wheeled out to sell and then brought back and locked up when the job was done.

The problem was that Sly was constantly recruiting my hawkers to

Stephanie Schnurr

help him after the game, and Sly is a demanding person to work for, which led to problems.

When Ilya first came to work for me he was clearly a young person in need of direction, and Sly was happy to provide direction. He turned Ilya into a servant. But when Ilya proved unwilling or incapable of doing the work to Sly's satisfaction, Sly soured on him, and proceeded to persecute him at every opportunity. I had to step in and remind Sly that although he could fire Ilya from his own business, he could not fire Ilya from mine — or bully him into quitting.

Likewise, Sly had Mike Cohen working for him after the games. Mike had been off and on with *Boston Baseball* for a couple of years, in between a stay in Israel. Sly took Mike on a trip to Cooperstown along with some of the other hawkers and ended up punching him in the face.

Sly giveth and Sly taketh away.

# 2008

April is the cruelest month. Every April there's a night that I come home, cold, wet and tired, and tell my wife that I'm sick of the ballpark, the magazine isn't selling, this year's hawkers are the worst bunch ever, and blah blah blah.

Well, 2008 was no different. But having made the necessary adjustments after the closing of Yawkey Way, and with *GameDay* calling it quits, we had a big year, our best ever for ballpark sales. It didn't feel like it at the time. We seemed to have more than our share of rain, and the hawkers gave me some trouble, but in the end the numbers were there, and another memorable postseason put us over the top.

It was an interesting season on the field as well. No sooner had we commemorated Manny Ramirez' 500th home run with a free postcard than the slugger was involved in altercations with Kevin Youkilis and with the team's traveling secretary. When he sat out several games pleading knee pain, the Red Sox demanded an MRI, calling his bluff. He was called on to pinch-hit against the Yankees, only to watch three called strikes from Mariano Rivera in a key at-bat.

Manny made some ill-advised complaints in the media, and his relationship with the front office entered a death spiral. Suddenly there was talk of dealing the slugger at the July 31 deadline.

I had just sent the August issue to the printer with Manny on the cover, so although I'd been calling on the team to dump him for years, I had mixed feelings when the Red Sox shipped Ramirez out in a three-team trade just before the deadline.

I felt good about the trade. It was probably the best that could be hoped for, given the way the situation had unraveled in the final week before the deadline. But I didn't feel too good about spending the month of August selling a magazine with Manny's photo on the cover when Manny was now playing for the Los Angeles Dodgers.

Players get traded at the deadline all the time, of course, but this had never happened to us in 19 years. It had happened to the Red Sox, though. Back in the days when they only published three issues each season, their third issue featured Danny Darwin on the cover even though "Dr. Death" had just undergone season-ending arm surgery. And they had to sell that cover for two months, not just one.

The Manny trade also left us with a stockpile of Manny-related bumper stickers, now useless. SupahFans had given us thousands of "Ortiz/Ramirez '08" and "Manny Being Marley" stickers, the latter portraying the deadlocked Ramirez in a pose reminiscent of the late Bob Marley.

To compensate for the poorly-timed cover, we wrote a story on the trade and printed it on the opposite side of the stat insert. As the month went on and Manny proceeded to tear up the National League, we updated the story with each visiting team, inserting it into every copy, and this seemed to satisfy almost everyone.

We also went to the well for new bumper sticker ideas. We did a second printing of the "YOOOOOUK!" stickers, which were very popular, and later a prescient "MVPEDROIA" sticker.

Boston's sophomore second sacker tore up the league in 2008, challenging for a batting title (.326), cranking 73 extra-base hits, knocking in 83 runs, and stealing 20 bases while only being caught once. He won the Gold Glove and was the AL's starting second baseman in the All Star Game.

Michael Cohen

Despite the efforts of Pedroia, the defending champions had a rough time of it in 2008. While Pedroia, Youkilis, Jon Lester and Daisuke Matsuzaka all turned in superlative seasons, Josh Beckett and David Ortiz struggled to stay healthy and effective, and after Ramirez was shipped out, the offense sputtered, especially on the road.

By late August, the Sox had squandered a couple of opportunities to make up ground on first-place Tampa, and it looked as if they might have to fight tooth and nail with Minnesota just to claim the wild-card berth.

I couldn't resist penning another column asking why it was that the Red Sox needed to spend $133 million in order to compete with Tampa ($44 million) and Minnesota ($57 million). In Tampa, it cost $137 to take a family of four to the ballgame. In Minnesota, $166. In Boston, a whopping $321. Sucker Nation indeed!

This time, I went the distance. I ordered two dozen blue caps with a red and white dollar sign on the front and 'Sucker Nation' embroidered on the back, and advertised them in the magazine.

My father hated this idea. So did many of the hawkers. And as it turned out, they were right. The Red Sox caught fire, challenged the Rays, and easily outdistanced the Twins for the wild card. As we know, when the team is winning, nobody cares about the other stuff.

Being stubborn, however, I wore my hat everywhere. I still do.

The last days of the season were disappointing. The Yankees were in town for a meaningless series and it was raining, which cost us the chance to sell out the September issue. We ended up with a split-admission double-header on Sunday, the last day of the season, and two of my hawkers went AWOL with their money, t-shirts, and aprons.

There have been a dozen such incidents over our 19 years at the ballpark. In almost every instance, it's been a hawker who has recently started working with us, sometimes on his very first day of work.

This time, however, it was two guys who had come to us as a pair. In 2006 and 2007 they had been handing out *GameDay* and they had seen my hawkers making good money, so when the 2008 season began they came to me and asked for jobs. They were marginal guys, living at the YMCA in Cambridge, but they had experience at the ballpark and I decided to give them a chance.

One of them came only sporadically as the season progressed, but the other became a regular hawker for us, a guy we got to know pretty well, who had shown us photos of his daughter in New York and whom we had all developed a liking for. So it was disappointing to all of us when, in the first of two games that Sunday, I sent them to the same gate and they talked each other into running off with the money.

It was a meaningless makeup game, sales were slow, and it wasn't a lot of money that they stole. It was nothing compared to the money they would have made if they had stuck around for the playoffs. It was one more bad decision by a couple of guys who have made many bad decisions in their lives.

When something like this happens, the hawkers want blood. They want to see me chase these guys to the ends of the earth. Me, I have mixed feelings about it.

On the one hand, I am a big believer in consequences. I also appreciate the example I set for the other hawkers by vigorously prosecuting thieves. And I've done it; I've spent many dreary hours at Roxbury District Court.

On the other hand, the legal system is slow and cumbersome, and even if I successfully prosecute a former hawker, I'm not going to get my money back. I'm just giving him a criminal record, or adding to the one he already has.

When a hawker steals from me, it pisses me off, but I also try to remember that most of these guys already have two strikes on them. Do I want to be the guy who yells "Strike three! You're OUT!"

No, I really don't.

Once again, the playoffs helped make our season. We got two ALDS home games as the Red Sox bested the Angels. We also got three ALCS home games as the Sox battled back from a 3-1 deficit against the Rays.

As it turned out, Game Five of the ALCS was the final Red Sox home game of the year. The Sox were down 3-1 in the series and had been blown out in Games Three and Four. The fans were downcast and sales were slow. By the time we were done counting out, the Red Sox were losing 5-0.

Chooch!

I told the guys I would see them in the spring, and I packed up my car with all the stuff that goes home for the winter — extra shirts, buttons, pencils, my bulletin board, the radio, and so on. I took everything home, and as I turned in to my driveway, the Rays scored two more runs to go up 7-0 in the top of the seventh.

If you don't remember what happened next, there are some great YouTube videos of the key hits that brought the Red Sox back. They scored four in the seventh, three more in the eighth, and J.D. Drew, of all people, had a walk-off RBI single in the bottom of the ninth to win it and send the series back to Tampa Bay.

The Red Sox won again in Tampa, setting up a winner-take-all seventh game. Back in Boxford, I worked all weekend to put together the World Series issue that would go to press first thing Monday morning if the Red Sox won. We'd get the magazines delivered on Wednesday for Game One of the World Series, here in Boston against the Phillies. Then I sat down Sunday night to watch the final game.

But the Red Sox lost, 3-1, and the season (theirs and ours) was over.

During the long baseball season, I'm too busy to think about the big picture. I've got a lot to do and I do it, checking off one item after another, being where I'm supposed to be, putting together the magazine and driving to the ballpark and counting out the hawkers and making sure we're ready to go for the next day, when we'll do it all again.

Then the offseason comes, with lots of down time to ponder what it all means.

I'm earning a living, but am I making a difference?

How do we explain the appeal of professional baseball, an archaic game played by mercenaries in pajamas?

What if our society could channel the energy we devote to pro sports into fighting ignorance, poverty, and disease?

There's a saying that if you love what you do, you'll never work a day in your life. I loved baseball, I made it my business, but now, twenty years later, it's just a business. It's become work.

In one sense, that's good. Having gone through that process gives me more perspective than some of the other folks who cover the Red Sox. And that's one of the elements that makes *Boston Baseball* unique.

In another sense, that's bad, because it's not fun any more. But I still take a tremendous amount of pride in what I have accomplished with *Boston Baseball*.

I built a business based on something I loved. I've given my fellow Red Sox fans a choice and saved them millions of dollars. I created jobs and opportunities for hundreds of people over the years. In attempting to manage those people, I learned a lot about myself. But finally and most importantly, I believe the magazine has been a positive influence in the lives of those who worked here the longest.

Boston Baseball: John, you're not from around here, and you didn't grow up a Red Sox fan. So, tell us a little bit about how you came to be living here and working for *Boston Baseball*.

John Freeman: I came up from Florida in 1970, and I lived in Kenmore Square. So I got to go into Fenway Park. And I started going to games. It was a buck a game back then, so I became a Red Sox fan. 1973, I started working down at Fenway Park, selling hot dogs and pretzels outside.

How I started working for *Boston Baseball*? Just like everyone else, I answered an ad, and came down.

BB: And you said, "I've done that."

JF: I've vended before, but this is a different type of vending. I had to adjust. It probably took me a half a year to realize that this is a different type of vending. Selling programs is different from selling pretzels and hot dogs. When you sell pretzels and hot dogs, there's more people that want those than want programs; you actually have to go out of your way to sell a program. You have to have a sales pitch. There are some people that want the program, but the majority of the people, you have to sell to. You have to give a little spiel.

BB: What year did you start working with us?

JF: Oh, I don't know, 2002, maybe. There were a lot of good salesmen back then. It was hard, as a rookie, to get good gates, so my numbers weren't that good. And it wasn't until the end of the year, when the people weren't making a lot of money and they started dropping off and not showing up, that I got good gates, and I started putting up good numbers. So the next year I had good gates and my numbers were excellent, you know.

BB: What do you remember about the guys who were working

John Freeman

here when you started?

JF: They were real aggressive! They had attitudes! They would probably knife their mother in the back, you know.

BB: Did you learn anything from those guys, or did you have to figure it out as you went along?

JF: I had to figure it out. It was just adjusting to my own style.

BB: How have things changed in the eight or nine years you have been working for *Boston Baseball*?

JF: The crowds have changed since then. There's a lot of first-time people coming to the park. Before, there were regular people who came every game. Now there's not. There's a lot of people asking where Gate A is, and they're standing in front of Gate A. You have to be polite about it.

BB: Why do you suppose that is?

JF: I think the people who have season tickets are now selling off their tickets because they can't afford to go to all the games. So the people who are coming to the games have never been to Fenway Park before. Even when they're at Fenway Park, they have no idea where they are. (Laughs) But you have to be polite, which we always are, and be hospitable.

BB: Southern hospitality.

JF: Absolutely!

BB: You have a very different delivery than some of the other guys who work here.

JF: Absolutely!

BB: And a different approach.

JF: I'd have it no other way. I have repeat customers because of that. They have come back to find me because I was nice, and did something nice. A couple of times I have people come back because I gave them a pencil. They say, "I wanted one but I was afraid to ask. And you said, 'Hey, would you like a pencil?'" Or, "I had two kids and you gave me an extra bumper sticker without me asking, and that was nice, so we come back to you." Even a year later!

BB: You're the only hawker who comes back in and says that he had a good time, or he talked to some nice people, or he had some good conversations.

JF: Yeah, well my goal here, every game I come down, is to meet four to ten good people every night. It's not to make money. It's to meet good people. We got 37,000 people coming to the ballpark, and I am here to meet great people every night, and that's what I do. That's my goal for every game.

BB: I was going to ask you what kept you coming back to *Boston Baseball* all these years. It's nice to have cash in your pocket. But you do seem to enjoy it for what it is.

JF: Absolutely! Well, I'm getting a little older and I'm getting a little more broken down. That's my goal now, to have a good time and to meet good folks! I mean, where else can you meet 37,000 people every night? You have a look around, and you're bound to meet good people. All you have to do is pay attention.

You see somebody staring, looking like they need help, you ask, "What are you looking for?" And you show them where it is. You be nice. Southern hospitality. They've never seen that up here before.

A lot of times, I get the comments, "You're different from the rest of the hawkers out here." I hear that on a regular basis the last three years, and I get those people coming back to me now.

BB: You've had some health problems in the last few years, and sometimes it's difficult for you just to walk down to the ballpark.

JF: Absolutely! (Laughs) I have a bad back. I have a broken bone in my back, and a pinched nerve, and a bulging disc, and I've had other problems, like an infection in my knee. It was rough walking. I couldn't walk from Kenmore Square to the ballpark without stopping three times. But I enjoy what I'm doing, so that's why I'm here. It's difficult, but once I get here, my adrenaline takes over, and it's fun to be here.

BB: And then do you pay for it later in the day?

JF: It's hard to get home! (Laughs) And I'm sure my wife's got to listen to my problems! She's got problems herself, you know. But I love to be down here. This is the mother church, you know, Fenway Park!

BB: In the years that you've worked here, what days stand out to you? Do you remember any particular days?

JF: Ahhh. When Ted Williams died. The World Series days — they were fun.

BB: You were a rookie hawker [when Ted Williams died]. What do you remember other than the fact that we made a lot of money?

JF: It was the first time I remember the crowd generating so much excitement — a feeding frenzy, you know. That was kind of interesting.

**175**

I try to make EVERY day a good day. I try to have that attitude where it's going to be a great day. Like today — it's pouring down rain, but I am going to make it a great day. I am going to try to have a good day. And try to make the people around me have a good day.

BB: How closely do you follow the team? Do you go home and watch the games with your wife?

JF: Absolutely!

BB: Do you read the magazine?

JF: Uh... (Laughs) I look through it, you know.

BB: What kind of role would you say *Boston Baseball* plays in your life?

JF: Besides giving me employment? I like being outside Fenway Park. It gives me some place to go. I can only be on my feet three and a half hours. And it's the right kind of job for me. It's what I can do. Like I said, I have some injuries. As far as that goes, it gives me a place in life to be right now.

There's people down here I like to be with. It's camaraderie, I guess. It's a nice place to hang out. There's new kids coming down and I like to try to show the new kids what's going on. Some of them don't want to listen, but you know!

BB: Now that Hai is not around all the time, you've kind of graduated into the role of being "the voice of reason," and the elder statesman here.

JF: That's sort of true. Yes, it is.

BB: By the end of the season, are you all done with the guys? Do you miss the guys over the winter? Or do you say, "Oh, God, I have to go back and deal with those idiots again!"

JF: No, it ain't that at all. I look forward to coming back! My wife doesn't look forward to me coming back! She's always asking me if this

is going to be my last year. I keep saying, "I don't think so!" I look forward to coming back.

This is actually fun for me to do. It gives me a REASON. I'm not ready to give up work. I'm not ready to let it go. I've been working since I was five years old. I love what I'm doing down here. I love Fenway Park. I love hanging at Fenway Park. Somebody gives me money for hanging out at Fenway Park! There's not a better job in the world! I would probably work for less money. But don't tell Mike that!

BB: Is there anything that you'd like to add?

JF: I would just like it to stop raining.

BB: I think it's lightening up now. Thank you, John.

Boston Baseball: You grew up here, as a Red Sox fan, playing baseball in East Boston...

Sly Egidio: I grew up playing baseball my whole life. I even played when I was in the military. I played all the way up until I was 30 years old and started my own company. Now I don't have time to do anything anymore.

But I grew up playing baseball, loving baseball. I used to sneak out of school all the time and come to games at Fenway, since I was 11 or 12 years old, take the train by myself, or with my friends from East Boston. When I was about 14 or 15 years old, that was when I started knowing my way around. I knew if I hung around outside the gates, I'd get a free ticket.

BB: Tell us what it was like when you first started working for *Boston Baseball*. Tell us about your first day; you like to tell that story.

SE: I couldn't find a job because I was 15 years old and minimum wage was like $3.50 an hour back in those days, but I had my working papers and I used to come to Fenway a lot and I'd ask all the guys "hey, how do I do this job?" And they gave me the runaround.

Finally somebody pointed me out to Mr. Rutstein, and you were selling at the ticket office I believe, and I walked up to you and I did have a Will Clark shirt on. I didn't have eye black on, but I had a Will Clark t-shirt and a Red Sox hat, and I asked you for a job.

You looked at me. I was really small back then, short and scrawny, and you said "Yeah, well..." and you gave me a cheesy business card and told me to give you a call. Well, I called you a few times, got the runaround, and I came back and eventually you gave me this two-page thing to fill out, and told me to come back again. Then one day, you're like "All right, take 40 books and go down past Gate D. Don't go to Gate D, because you know, someone is selling there, don't interfere with him."

Sylvester "Sly" Egidio

BB: So on your first day, you basically got sent to the bus stop on Boylston Street?

SE: I didn't even have a gate! After about 10 or 15 minutes I sold a few, but I thought about it and figured out that the harder I work, the more I sell, the more I sell the more I make — all right, this is a pretty good thing. So I started selling, and I believe I sold just a few less than the guy at Gate D. I know you always say the number goes up every time I tell the story, but in reality, I think I sold 100 books that day, and the guy at the Gate D only sold 140. I must have done something right, because Mike looked at the numbers and he paid me and he said, "Make sure that you're here at 4:00 tomorrow... you got the job." Then I came back and I did a couple of more games, and my sales started to go up, and I started to learn how to sell.

BB: What do you remember about the guys who were working for the magazine back then?

SE: (Laughs) It was an older crowd, rough older guys, guys that were using it as a second job to pay their bills because they had wives and kids and things like that. And I was a 15-year-old rookie and these

179

guys were all in their late teens, early twenties and even out of school or college — married with facial hair, you know — and I'm this kid who collects baseball cards. It was tough working with all those older guys. I got hazed a lot, messed around with, but I learned a lot too, just by watching people and getting better.

BB: Who messed with you?

SE: (Laughs) None of them messed with me, really, it was just the same rookie hazing we do even to this day. I don't think I started until May of 1992, or maybe the end of April. I think the first issue I sold was Mo Vaughn and Frank Thomas back to back, and the cover wasn't glossy, but it was color.

BB: What else do you remember about the magazine from back then? I know that you keep copies of the back issues, so you know better than anybody how far the magazine has come.

SE: What I remember most was that you were very concerned with it, very focused on it, even before you quit your job to do it full time. But it was your heart and soul at the time, and you'd give it 110%, and so would all the workers. It was almost like a call to arms, like "we're battling the Red Sox, help us out!" And all the workers were really into it.

The magazine was just black and white pages with a color cover, that was it. I remember when we first got the color glossy cover. I remember how it grew to all glossy. I remember when it went up to two dollars, I remember the All Star game, the World Series. We're talking 20 years and I was there for 18 of them, so yeah, I remember a good portion, almost everything.

BB: You were there on the front line when the Red Sox and Code Enforcement tried to shut us down — you were the guy who came running back to the office and told me that Richie Iannella was up at Gate D giving Aaron a hard time, and that was how it all started.

SE: Yeah, I think we knew we were at war then, you recognized what you had to do to make the magazine better, but you also knew you had to get good hawkers. We were out there day in and day out: "Programs! Scorecards! Don't read about the May Sox, pick up the June

*Baseball Underground.*" Things like that.

I remember the Harry M. Stevens guys with their kiosks out front, causing problems for us, yelling at us, swearing at us. I got a ham sandwich thrown at me by a Harry M. Stevens guy. I remember I'd be making a sale, and they'd run right up in front of me and say "No, no, no. You want this one!"

I think their tactics were one of the reasons why so many fans bought our magazine. The Red Sox were saying, "Oh, he's tricking the fans" but it was nothing like that. It's a good product at a good price, and we're just out there selling it. And these guys would push us out of the way, throw things at us, swear at us... really mean, vulgar and rude. And the fans saw that, and of course they bought from the 16-year-old kid who's working hard and just needs some money for school.

BB: It really was a competition every day between our guys and their guys, much more so than it is now.

SE: I think people forget. You and I, we're the only two people left in the company now that remember that day-in and day-out, that's all the focus was: the competition. We have to sell more than them! Inside they were like, "We have to beat *Baseball Underground*! We have to destroy *Baseball Underground.*" It was war. Business is war. And there we were, on the front lines.

BB: Do you actually read the magazine?

SE: Cover to cover. I always have. If you quiz me on it, I can tell you anything about it. I mean, I'm a baseball fan! I love baseball. Baseball is my life. I own a company that deals with baseball; I work for another one. That's all I do. Fenway Park is what I do, full time.

BB: What's the first thing you read when the magazine comes out?

SE: The first thing I look at is my advertisers, as I have quite a few of them in there. I want to make sure that my advertisers are happy! Business first, always. Then I go to the minor league report, I look at the stats, because for my business, Beantown Collectibles, I need to know what's going on in the minors. That's something that *Boston Baseball* has always been on top of.

**181**

BB: What's in the magazine that you look at and think, "Why the hell does Mike have this in the magazine?"

SE: To be honest, I don't really see any problem with the magazine at all. I guess maybe there could be some more pictures in there. And I could maybe get some more advertisers in there, but other than that...

I've been around the country, I've worked for *Chicago Baseball*, I ran *Ballpark Monthly* in Atlanta, this is what I do. I think you and I have a better idea than anyone of what it takes to make and sell a successful game program.

BB: Tell us more about working in Chicago and Atlanta with Jay Roper's publications.

SE: After winning three MVPs with *Boston Baseball*, I enlisted in the military and did that for a while. I was coming into reserve status and looking for a job, and I got offered several jobs, one in Baltimore, one in Chicago and one in Cleveland, all with alternative baseball publications. I used Mike Rutstein and *Baseball Underground* as a model, and as a reference. And people knew who I was. People have come to the ballpark and watched me sell! They knew what kind of seller I was, and they wanted me to replicate that for them.

I went out there and did very well, and was extremely successful everywhere. However, I think the one thing that we had here with *Boston Baseball* was strong leadership at the top in the guy who made the magazine and put it together, and also on the battlefield which is the streets. We had strong hawkers who were knowledgeable, knew what they were doing, knew how to sell the product, and showed up every game. That's hard to find elsewhere in the country.

BB: You've worked over a thousand games for *Boston Baseball*. What days stand out to you?

SE: For me, the only two things I've ever done is work the ballpark and defend my country, and I can tell you that the passing of Ted Williams, those two days... the day he actually passed and then the day they held the service for him at the ballpark... so many people know I idolized the guy,. Fans were coming up to me, shaking my hand, hugging me, buying the program because it had a special commemorative

card.... buying five, buying ten.

But the fans, and I think this is the beginning of when MY fan base really started... the fans sought me out all around the park, walked around looking for me, to hug me and see if I was all right, buy a program off me. That sticks out.

The day they had the service at Fenway Park for Ted, I came in after selling an immense amount of our commemorative programs. I came in and cashed out with you. You said, "Where are you going? You've got Gate A tonight, you're on a roll!" I said, "There's something I have to do." And I left, and I came back a few hours later in dress blues, with the rest of my Marines, and you said "Ah, I understand." And you shook my hand and everything. That was pretty cool.

That was a time I think you said, "Ah, he's grown up. He's a man now." I thought that was pretty cool. Those two days stick out very much for me.

BB: Obviously you've got other irons in the fire; you don't need to be here selling magazines every day. It's a young man's job. What keeps you coming back?

SE: I've asked veteran ballplayers that: "How come you stay in baseball?" I guess when you love the game, you love the sport, you love being at the ballpark... I mean, there's good things and bad things, but I just love being down here.

At this stage of my life I have so much going on. My company is growing and in another year or two I'm going to have an office and a warehouse. I see myself five or ten years from now, leaving my office early and telling my secretary, "All right, I'll see you when I see you." I'll come down to the park and just sell programs. It's funny because somebody will look at me, maybe give me a hard time, and they will have no clue that I'm the president of a MAJOR company. That's my goal.

BB: How about ten years from now? Where will you be? You'll be in your forties, like I am now.

SE: I don't think Mike Rutstein thought he would be in his forties working at *Boston Baseball!* I don't think you foresaw that you'd be out here for twenty years, that this magazine would be recognized across the country. People know what this magazine is!

I don't think you understood that his magazine would be a collectible. I see them online, autographed, or not even autographed, for $10, $15, even $20. They were one-dollar and two-dollar publications. It's twenty years! We are part of Red Sox history! We're going to live forever!

BB: We talked about moments that stand out for you; how about some of the people who've worked for *Boston Baseball* that stand out for you?

SE: Wow! There's been a lot of bad ones... people who would go out for two hours and sell four or five programs, and then lose the money. (Laughs) And then we've had some great hawkers.

I tend to remember the good and great ones because I've had to battle them for sales supremacy and it's really hard to come in every day, day in and day out, and give 110% and sell. I remember the guys that won homestands, the guys that beat me for homestands, the guys I had to go up against. You remember the competitive nature of those guys, the competition, that's what I remember most.

BB: Who — after yourself — is the best hawker in the history of *Boston Baseball?*

SE: That would be Ryan Goldney, because in order to be considered a great salesman, you have to do it consistently. And he did it consistently: he did it as a rookie, he did it in the late '90s before it went to two dollars and the hawkers were selling five to six hundred per game because they were a dollar. After it turned to two dollars, he came in at the tail end of the battle with the Red Sox, he watched it change into a glossy publication, he battled me in the 2000, 2002.

Also, he came back in 2003, which was a big year for us. The Red Sox were amazing, but the company was low on good hawkers because I was away at war for fourteen months and didn't work a single game; and it was a time when a lot of the older guys moved on, got married, left. A lot of the good hawkers were gone. He came back and I won't say "saved it," but definitely came in and changed things and people saw that it WAS possible to sell 200 or 300 books at this gate. He was definitely a spark of energy, and he kept things going. He was the right man at the right time in 2003.

BB: How many runners have you had in eighteen years? A dozen?

SE: Chad was a good runner. He's not with us any longer, he passed away. Coolidge was a good runner, that was in the '90s. There was this tall, crazy Italian black guy, Frank, he was a good runner. I was young, 14, 15, 16, and Frank would talk to you, tell you what you were doing right and wrong. You know, the runner is like the catcher. You're on the mound and you're going to win 20 games, but it helps to have a good runner.

The runner we have now, and that we had a couple of years ago, is Ryan DiGiacomo. He left for a while. Over the winter I approached him on numerous occasions and begged him to come back as the runner. This year, he's done it all for me, for Mike, for everyone. He's probably gonna win MVP. I tell you, he has my vote.

BB: You haven't mentioned two of the guys who are really at the heart and soul of *Boston Baseball*, Hai and Lemon.

SE: Well, Hai and Lemon are gone now, but they come back from time to time, and I am sure they will appear again. They were young guys in the '90s like myself, just a couple of years behind me. They understood hard work and determination; they understood everything.

Ryan DiGiacomo

These guys came from far away, took the train, went home late at night, and did it all again the next day.

Hai, Lemon, myself, Ryan, there's a bunch of guys that at pivotal points showed up and were like the cavalry coming over the hill. I think it helped you when these guys came and just could do anything you asked them to do. We needed someone to stuff, we needed someone to run, we needed someone to sell, it didn't matter, they did it.

BB: You were here when we first battled with the Red Sox back in the early 1990s, and then again 15 years later we had to face another serious challenge from the *Metro*. What do you remember about that?

SE: I remember what we went through when Aramark took over, I think it was 2000 or 2001, and the *Metro* came soon after. But at that point we were so established — you don't want to attack an entrenched, well-fortified opponent. By then, *Boston Baseball* was a household name, and they didn't think it through when they decided to come out on the street and compete with us. I remember them coming out after the new ownership had taken over, and then they saw how embarrassing it was for them within a month. They gave up quicker than the old regime did.

But what they did was, they went out and hired the *Metro*, for a lot of money, to put us out of business! I mean, that's like hiring somebody else to do your fighting! Did the *Metro* really care? The people the *Metro* hired didn't even care! I saw them throwing those *GameDay* things in the dumpster. You don't see *Boston Baseball* employees throwing the magazines away! You walk around Fenway Park, you don't see this in the trash. *GameDay* was being thrown in the dumpster at night by the bundle! I don't think they thought it through. It cost them a lot of money, though.

BB: Talk a little bit about this business you've started. You're very organized with your carts and the items you sell after the games, and you're selling online now as well.

SE: When I got home from the conflict in 2004 I came back to *Boston Baseball*, and toward the end of '04 I had this vision. I said, you know, I'm getting older, I've done a lot in my life and I've done a lot to help other people, I've served my country twice. I said, I'm going to start doing things for ME. I came up with the idea for this company. I got in bed with all the official licensing for MLB, the NFL, all four sports, and I think that also strengthened not only Beantown Collectibles, but the whole *Boston Baseball* thing.

BB: Obviously, you've spent a long time selling stuff outside the ballpark, and you also worked for a while for both Twins and Sportsworld. What's it like selling after the game? How is that different?

SE: It's pretty much the same, though the crowd's a little wilder. There are a lot of drunks.

I've seen it all change. I've seen what this place is like. I remember working out of a van with *Baseball Underground* when the Red Sox were trying to stay out of last place with the Brewers and the Indians. There were about 12,000 fans in this ballpark, and tickets were free! People would give me stacks of them! Nowadays, a tour of the ballpark, when the Sox aren't even in town and there's no game, is $12 for a ticket! I've seen it all change, I've seen it all come and go.

After the game, you have the same problems as you do before the game. You have a little bit of a rowdy crowd, but the fans are the fans. The real fans know us, just like they know their program salesman.

I've been at Gate A for almost 20 years and I've seen so many people. My fans! I have fans that come up to me and ask me for my baseball card. They bake me cookies, bring me pizzas, give me ski trips, give me $100 gift certificates, free lift and rental to a ski place — I don't even ski! They gave me VISA gift cards the last few years. People hand me VISA gift cards they bought with their hard-earned money! They don't even know me and I don't know them by name! I'm the programsman!

The fans, that's what keeps me coming back. I know so many people! I get immense amounts of positive feedback, I can't even tell you, I can't even begin to describe it.

I remember in '06 when the season ended on a sour note, and I'm leaving, people were walking up to me and hugging me. They knew I felt bad. I was sitting there just watching people leave and people were coming up to me and shaking my hand, and every day when you have a bad day, or it's raining or you're in a bad mood, someone will come up to you with their kids and say, "You're in our video, will you sign this for us, will you take a picture with us?" and it makes you feel good.

BB: What do you want to add? Your kids are going to read this book someday!

SE: I know they are! When I came here, I was 15 years old, and you had just gotten out of college. And now look at us! We're old!

I see people coming to the ballpark, I've seen their kids grow up and now their kids are coming to the ballpark on dates! Driving here, with their own car, on dates! I'm like, I can't believe I'm still here! But you just see so much and you are part of so much.

I guess I want to say thank you to the fans, all the people that bought programs from me. All the people I've met at the ballpark over the years.

My mother has scrapbooks full of my pictures and the DVDs and newspaper articles and so on that I've been in. It amazes me that I'm just a program guy, but anywhere I go, someone recognizes me. I was in a foreign country once, coming home, and I was on the tarmac with my troops, and these Air Force guys walked up to me as we were getting ready to board a plane back to the States, and this guy goes "Are you from Boston by any chance, Marine?" And I said "Yes, why do you ask?"

He said, "You wouldn't happen to work at Fenway Park, would you?" And I start laughing because the furthest thing from my mind was Fenway Park. I've got a rifle on my back and we're thousands of miles away from the United States, and these two guys wanted to shake my hand because I was the program guy.

Things like that have happened to me every city I go to: Baltimore, San Diego. During the 2007 World Series, I'm walking in and some guy ran up to me and had to have his picture taken with me and his wife and kid. He had never seen the Red Sox win a World Series, he had missed it in '04 and he was so excited. He was like "That's the Program Guy! That guy is a legend at Fenway Park! He's in all my movies!" You know, things like that, you don't know what to say. You shake their hand and sign their autographs, and it humbles you.

I remember talking to players about it. Trot Nixon, Nomar Garciaparra, Kevin Youkilis, Bronson Arroyo, so many guys I know personally. I remember Nomar said, "Your fans are everything."

Trot Nixon said to me once, "You're going to live in Red Sox lore forever. You're going to live forever in Red Sox lore because you're in the '04 and '07 Red Sox World Series videos. You will always be that 20-something Program Guy with the goatee, even 50 years from now! That's the thing about Boston. You're like a ballplayer, you've got rock star status now!"

It goes to your head sometimes. But when you're walking down the street and people are like, "Hey, you need a ride?" Or "Hey, you're the Program Guy! I want my wife to meet you!"

It just grew into something we never thought it would be. Twenty years? We never thought it would be like this in a million years!

Boston Baseball: I've been starting out by asking people if they were Red Sox fans and did they play Little League growing up, but your childhood wasn't like that.

Hai Ho Nguyen:  No, it wasn't.  It was a little different.  I came to the States when I was about eight years old.  I lived in Dorchester and grew up in Brookline, thanks to Section 8. Yes.

BB:  When did you first know there was something called baseball?

HHN:  I heard about baseball from a couple of kids in Dorchester. My cousin lived very close to a baseball card store, around the corner from where he lives.  His friends that he made across the street were a couple of white kids that collected baseball cards.  So, when I went to visit him from the other side of the neighborhood, he introduced me to the kids.  We got along well, and one day when they went to the baseball card shop, they brought us all along.

I was like, "This is some fun!"  I just started to buy packs of baseball cards from the stores.  I liked the mystery of it, not knowing which players I was going to get.

BB:  How did you know which players were good?

HHN:  I was relying on my friends to know these things.  What little I knew about it was through TV.  There wasn't much to do other than watch TV, even though I didn't understand the language.

When I moved to Brookline, I got into the Michael Driscoll Middle School. I was assigned to a special student teacher who loved baseball.  She invited her boyfriend one day to a game.  Her boyfriend couldn't go, so she offered the extra ticket to me.  We both went to the game.

We were sitting out in the bleachers, and that was the first time that I got a little bit of an understanding as to why I was collecting baseball cards and who these players were, even though I had watched

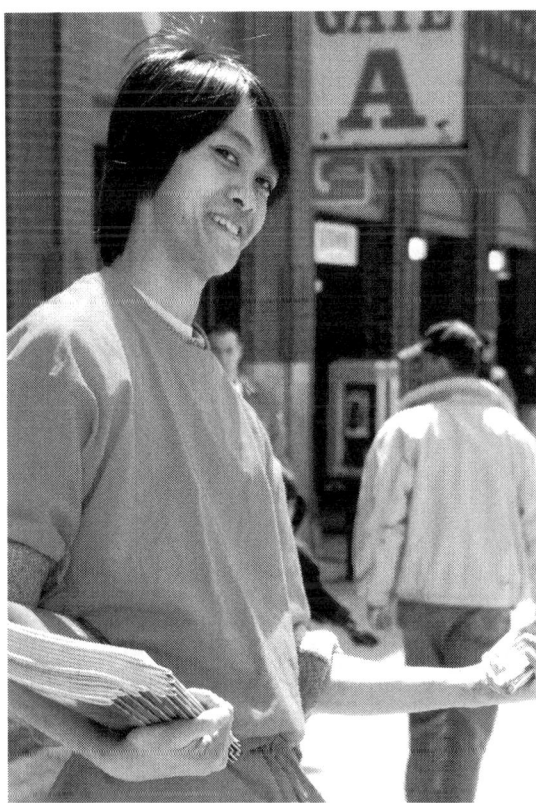

Hai Ho Nguyen

them on TV.

I was just interested in hanging out with these kids, buying these cards, and watching it on TV because it was fun and it gave me a sense of belonging because I didn't have many friends. When you come into the States, all you have is your family. My family didn't have much of a range in terms of friends. We stuck together. When they introduced me to those other kids, I just wanted to be like them. So I went and bought cards and got into that, but I didn't know much about it until that time when the student teacher brought me to Fenway Park.

BB: How old were you?

HHN: I was in the 5th or 6th grade. I had to be at least 12 years old.

BB: How was your English then?

HHN: It wasn't good.

BB: Could you understand what was going on?

HHN: No. It was this giant stadium! We walked around the entire stadium to see what it was like. We went to our seats in the bleachers. I was just in awe of the size of the place and the crowd, the people. I had never seen so many! I didn't understand anything about the game, how it was played or anything like that, but I liked it. I liked the atmosphere. I loved every moment of it.

So, when I went home, I had a lot of wonderful dreams about it. I always meant to come back. When summer came, I went down to the ballpark by myself on the C line, which ran next to my house on Washington Street. I didn't tell my parents. I just hopped on the T and went down to Fenway and just really was looking. I walked all around the ballpark. It was really early in the afternoon. I brought a baseball, a used baseball that I played with. It was one of these cheap baseballs that you could get at Woolworth's. There used to be a Woolworth's in Brookline!

I brought it down. I was just playing around with it. I had no concept of getting an autograph. But I saw a bunch of kids running around chasing players. They were asking for autographs. I was just curious, I was like, "Wow, this is fun."

BB: This is down at Gate D?

HHN: This was down at Gate D, and then I took out my baseball. I didn't have a pen. My first autograph was Roger Clemens!

Back then there was not all the security hoopla that they have nowadays. The players just drove in or walked in like normal Joes. This was in the early 1990s. Really, the Red Sox were a shit team. No one cared. The fence was unblocked. Nowadays it's blocked because they want their privacy. You could see the players walking from the entrance all the way into the clubhouse. I saw Roger Clemens walking in. I was like, "Mister, can you sign this thing?" I had no idea who he was. Some kid next to me had a Sharpie, so Clemens signed it with that Sharpie. That really sticks in my mind.

BB: What happened to that baseball?

HHN: That baseball came back to the house. I played with it. I really didn't care. Do you know what? Roger Clemens wasn't the only autograph I got that day. I was running around getting all these guys' autographs just because the other kids were doing it. My last autograph that day was Don Mattingly. He pulled up in a cab. He came out, and everybody rushed up to him and asked for an autograph. I was his last kid. I asked him, "Mister, can you sign this?" He was like, "Okay, whatever."

BB: You had Mattingly and Clemens on the same ball, and you took it home and played with it?

HHN: I didn't care. I didn't know much about any of these people. I just wanted to be part of something fun, and there were kids that were my age that thought it was good.

BB: Tell me how you started working for *Boston Baseball*.

HHN: I found out through my buddy, John Ovesen — people knew him as Lemon. He was one of those kids who was running around getting autographs. That entire summer, I kept coming back whenever there was a game. I saw all these kids getting autographs. He was the one that seemed to be the most talkative, the easiest to approach. So I tried to make friends as much as I could with him. One day I saw him going in and out of the garage. I didn't think about it. The next day there was a game and I saw him working outside of Fenway, selling programs. I was like, "That looks like fun." So I asked him, "What are you doing? Do you think I can do that too?"
He pointed out this place and told me to talk to the boss and see where it goes. So, I walked into —

BB: This is the pizza place, Mom & Pop's?

HHN: Yes. I asked you, "Do you think I can work here?" You said, as far I remember, "Sure. What can you do?" I told you, "I can do anything." And you told me to come back the next day. I came back the next day, and you gave me something to do.

BB: Running, stuffing, selling?

HHN: I think I was running, the day when I started. For that entire week I was there, delivering programs or selling programs and doing whatever you needed me to do. I was just this funny little kid. I really didn't want to challenge anybody. I liked the atmosphere, so I stayed. I didn't really say too much. I just did what I could. Yes.

BB: You liked the atmosphere. What was it like? Who were the guys who were working there that you remember?

HHN: I remember a lot of people. I remember the Wizard, Jeff Brink. Sylvester Egidio, a little scrawny Italian kid, loud mouth. I remember Lisa, a beautiful girl. She was a lot older than I was. I remember Michael, Johan, I remember the Chico Brothers. It was a cast of characters that I really enjoyed because of how they expressed themselves — very freely and openly. I've always felt that I am a free spirit. I know that now more than I did before, but I felt that personal connection. That's why I stayed. There were a lot of people that were really, really interesting when I started.

BB: What was the magazine like back then?

HHN: You know, the magazine has come a long a way. The magazine was really a beat up, crappy, colorless book! When I picked up those few first early issues, and I read it, I didn't fully understand everything. But it didn't look like a professional program like we have now. We have everything fully glossy. It's 20 years in the making, and it's a lot better. We came a long way. In the beginning it looked like a newsletter-type thing that you never expected to buy, but once you pick it up, and I've spoken to a lot of fans, "Why would you want to buy these things?" and they're like, "It speaks to me. This is exactly how I feel toward the team." Back then it wasn't really a good Red Sox team. Most people just wanted an objective point of view.

BB: You were a regular for over 10 years with *Boston Baseball*. Of all the days you worked at the ballpark, which ones stand out for you?

HHN: Back then we did a lot of cruel things to people, especially those who were smaller, younger and new to the company. I thank God that the guys, the older ones, really didn't have any clue what I was. I think they just wanted to leave me alone.

There were these two kids that they called the Chico Brothers. One day the older hawkers took out one of these duffle bags that you get in the military, and they stuffed them in the bag and carried them up to Gate A and rolled them around and kicked them and ran away. I thought that was the most —

BB: Whose idea was that?!?

HHN: That idea actually came from Sly and Coolidge, taunting the rookies. I thought that was amusing even though it had nothing to do with selling programs.

BB: Give me another one, one that doesn't involve physical violence.

HHN: There was a day recently that I really liked. John Freeman was on the bridge. We sold an enormous amount of programs that day, so many that we had lost track of how many programs we had sold. Freeman was on the bridge and he thought maybe he had broken the record. Freeman had so much money that he asked me to put it in a box and run it back to Mike because he couldn't hold it all!

We figured out at the end of the day that he broke the record not by one or two but by a large margin.

I remember one time when the Red Sox were in the playoffs. I don't remember what year it was, but it was a best-of-five series, and the Red Sox went down by two games. Everybody thought the Red Sox would be eliminated, and half the sellers, led by Tim Michaud, had driven up to New Hampshire. They didn't think that the Red Sox would have another home game. But they did, and you had only three to four guys, and I was out there trying to run and sell at the same time!

It was the most difficult time I ever had, but I tried to manage by hiding the books next to a trash barrel. Every time somebody needed books, I stopped selling and ran over to give them the programs they needed and then came back to my spot and sold. Still, on that particular day, I sold a lot! It was the playoffs, and people were buying these books like hotcakes. I had to sell and run at the same time while being able to hide these books so that people wouldn't steal them. I was going out of my mind that night. I was hoping that Tim would come back. He never did!

BB: All those years you were at the ballpark, you had opportunities to do other things. You had other jobs, and you did a lot of traveling. What kept you coming back to the ballpark?

HHN: The reason why I come back to the ballpark, besides being with the guys, is that I really enjoy being at Fenway Park where you see all kinds of people, talk to all types of people, and you're able to figure out a little bit more about yourself.

At first I was scared. The first day I was selling programs, I was nervous about people looking at me. Over the years, I realized that you really don't have anything to be nervous about. These people are just here to have fun. When you can see that, it makes you feel like it's worthwhile. Also, the thing is that I just like the atmosphere that is around the place. I like the work. Yes.

BB: How would you describe the guys here at the ballpark?

HHN: Oh, man, they are a weird group of people! These people came from very different backgrounds. But when they come here, it feels like they're in a place where they're comfortable. It's the same feeling that I get when I come here.

If you were a writer and you came by and interviewed these guys, you could literally write a book about them. One time my buddy Lemon was robbed coming home from Fenway. He had $24 on him. He was extremely young. He had a gun pushed in his face. He was told to give up whatever money he had in his pocket. He gave it to them, and luckily he came out alive. He came back to the ballpark the next day, and he was completely freaked out. I chased him down the street and told him to relax. I didn't know exactly what had happened. This is one of those things that these people have for backgrounds that are very interesting.

When we all come together to sell programs, everyone can see that we are very strong individuals in certain ways. I don't think these people break that easily. If they do break, it would be a very little just because they need to get over the shock. Then they'll come out all right. I think that's true. They're strong individuals that would be able to hold still

Hai, wearing his runner's hat

when something bad happens because it's not like their life has been very smooth. It's like Sylvester Egidio. His childhood wasn't easy. You can see all that. He's extremely strong. We can respect that. That's why we work together. We're like a working family; we understand who we are.

We have guys who have no fathers, whose fathers beat them up, we don't say much about it. We all have those problems. We still are able to respect each other because every one of us is strong. I think everyone comes here to be in a group of people that know who we are, what we're like, what our backgrounds are like. When we go out and sell programs, we leave all that behind. When we don that *Boston Baseball* shirt, we feel like we're different people, and it seems to have some sort of simple power. We don't need to be these people that we are in the rest of our lives.

That's the comfort that I get when I come to the ballpark. Not only is it going to see these great friends and going to talk to these people who go to the game, but these people that I work with who are making this great escape from their day-to-day lives.

BB: You and Lemon used the money that you made at *Boston*

*Baseball* to travel all over the world. That's pretty cool.

HHN: I think so. If it wasn't for *Boston Baseball*, I would have never traveled. If it wasn't for *Boston Baseball*, I would have never had a good understanding as to why the world goes around. I think if it wasn't for *Boston Baseball*, I would have just been another sick, Asian kid who goes to college and had a regular job. *Boston Baseball* gave me a huge world of understanding.

I grew up in Brookline, very isolated. I lived in a neighborhood that is very, very well off. I went to a school that is very, very well groomed. Working for *Boston Baseball*, I met all these kids from Revere, Southie and East Boston, bad neighborhoods that don't have great schools or great parents. These kids showed me how to talk to people who are smart in a street way, but maybe not educated.

If it wasn't for the money that I was making at the ballpark, I wouldn't have been able to be independent within my own home. When you come here and live on Section 8, you obviously have parents that don't have any money. You're not going to ask them for allowance. Allowance is unheard of in Vietnam. *Boston Baseball* provided me financial independence so that my parents didn't have to worry about me. The money I earned, I saved it and I used it to travel. I visited a lot of places around the world, which added to more of my understanding of the world, which reinforced what I learned here in *Boston Baseball*. If it wasn't for *Boston Baseball*, I wouldn't be able to visit twenty- or thirty-something countries. It was a great, great place that I owe a lot of debt and gratitude to.

Travel has been very dear to me because traveling gives me a sense of who I am, why I'm here. It gives me an understanding as to why my parents came to the States. I think it helps me understand where I need to go next in life. A large part of that began with *Boston Baseball*, the money that I made there, and the friends that I made there. I did travel a lot. I'm very grateful for it.

BB: How do you think things have changed around the ballpark in the 14 or 15 years since you first started coming here?

HHN: When I started out, there were a lot of very enthusiastic people going to the games. People knew the stats. If you challenged them as to who had how many RBIs last year or this year, who wears this number, or who had how many home runs, they knew it.

Now it's very corporate; not only that, it's a lot of people who just think that Fenway is a nice place to go and watch some entertainment. Yes, it's a very entertaining game, but it's because of these people that the ballpark has become so expensive that the fans that I really liked before are not able to afford it.

Nowadays it's just like you go to the game, and you want to have a couple of drinks and talk to your friends while you're twittering away and saying, "It was a great game. You should have been here." Yes, yes. You could have all done that in your basement without paying anything.

I don't despise them. It's not like I don't like them. It's just that I miss the people who would be wearing their Red Sox shirts that they've had since their college years and maybe are able to still fit into and bring their kids to the game. Those are the guys I want.

I remember one game when the Yankees came in. This was when the Yankees weren't winning so much. For this particular game, there were a group of Hispanic fans that had come up from the Bronx wearing Yankees flags like capes. They had a drummer out there, and people clapping behind them, and there was a train of 20 to 25 people following them around the ballpark yelling about how the Yankees were coming to town. That's the atmosphere I want!

.

Made in the USA
Charleston, SC
22 August 2015